Lessons Along the Way

Lessons Along the Way

BEFORE, DURING AND
AFTER THE PRIESTHOOD

Richard C. Keil

Copyright © 2015 Richard C. Keil
All rights reserved.

ISBN: 1511949686
ISBN 13: 9781511949682
Library of Congress Control Number: 2015906835
CreateSpace Independent Publishing Platform
North Charleston, South Carolina

Acknowledgement

SPECIAL THANKS TO MY FRIEND, Colleen McMillar, who edited this book, reorganized it when necessary and never stopped prodding me to provide more details.

Note from Author

IT IS NOT MY INTENTION to hurt, embarrass or bring unwanted attention to anyone as I attempt to write about my life and the valuable lessons I've learned in my 80-some years on earth. In some instances, names have been changed to protect the privacy of those who unwittingly have become a part of my tale.

Contents

Acknowledgement v
Note from Author vii
Foreword. xi
Preface xix
Lessons from Early Life. 1
   Chapter 1 3
   Chapter 2 15
   Chapter 3 28
Lessons from the Seminary. 51
   Chapter 4 53
   Chapter 5 66
   Chapter 6 75
   Chapter 7 85
   Chapter 8 96
   Chapter 9 118
   Chapter 10 125
   Chapter 11 129
   Chapter 12 134
   Chapter 13 144

Lessons from the Priesthood 155
    Chapter 14 157
    Chapter 15 178
    Chapter 16 194
    Chapter 17 202
    Chapter 18 208
    Chapter 19 220
    Chapter 20 224
    Chapter 21 229
    Chapter 22 241
    Chapter 23 249
    Chapter 24 254
    Chapter 25 261
    Chapter 26 271
    Chapter 27 278
Lessons Along the Way 283
    Chapter 28 285
    Chapter 29 291
    Chapter 30 298
    Chapter 31 305
    Chapter 32 314
    Chapter 33 319
    Chapter 34 324
    Chapter 35 330
    Chapter 36 341
Afterword 347

Foreword

ONCE IN A GREAT WHILE, a story is told that enlarges our consciousness and animates new capacities for spiritual awakening. The stories that Richard Keil tells in *Lessons Along the Way* are compelling precisely because they enlarge our awareness of human possibility.

By opening himself to the grace of learning from those who appear in his life as friend, as foe, as intimate or as stranger, he gleans lessons that mobilize us toward fuller expressions of our own humanity. Specifically, his stories reveal our inextricable connectedness to other beings.

Perhaps it starts with opening to grace. How otherwise do we travel the journey from Sheboygan, Wisconsin, with young white boy who kneeled to pray for goodness and justice in the world to Holy Trinity, Alabama, where the young white priest kneeled eye to eye with a young black girl to help her envision a life free of violence, deprivation, and despair?

The journey that unfolds in *Lessons Along the Way* is marked with revelations about the paradox of power: power as an authentic spiritual calling and power that exists primarily to perpetuate itself. It was probably the latter that troubled the soul of the young boy we first meet in Sheboygan. Power, in its most elemental sense, is that magnificent energy that allows us to influence and be influenced by others. In a world marred by schisms of every sort, we most often encounter power, not as grace, but as a marker of culturally sanctioned inequality. This distortion of power may be most accurately described as "power-over." It is the distortion of power that breeds the injustice, violence and oppression that all too often come to be seen as normal. We sum it up as "that's just the way the world works."

One of the revelations of Keil's journey is that power-over depends for its existence upon remaining hidden in plain sight. It follows then that the journey toward fulfilling our spiritual calling begins with naming power-over for what it is.

The stories in *Lessons Along the Way* are all the more instructive because they reveal the possibilities that surface when we refuse to surrender our right to see, to engage and to imagine. One of the markers of a power-over organization is that its "practitioners" reserve for themselves the right to define reality. They get to say what is real, what is right, what is possible. Working within the rigid hierarchies of the Catholic Church, Keil encountered this practice, often tragically, on an everyday basis. It is, in fact, this practice that allowed pedophilia and child molestation to rage unabated and unchallenged; indeed, protected by the Church.

So long as the entitlements of the holy orders are presumed unimpeachable, one risks threats of condemnation and exclusion if he or she dares to call out the alcoholism, the violence, the moral malfeasance, and even the *sufferings* of clergy. In fact, as Keil discovered, to call out the violations of power-over for what they are, to expose the vast destructiveness of an ego-absorbed hierarchy is to risk being called crazy.

People do not awaken easily from the *un*-consciousness of power-over, because in large part, to awaken is to confront our fears. The fears that breed in power-over cultures (be they family, church or societal) blunt the imaginations of the dominators and the dominated alike. One of the marvels of our time is that 21st century neuroscience is offering incontrovertible evidence of what the ancient prophets and wisdom teachers have always proclaimed: that we are made to thrive in connection with each other; that we become most fully human through engagement with each other. As Martin Buber would put it, that the purpose of our being is *interbeing*. In a culture built on the illusion of our separateness, power-over thrives through the perpetuation of institutions and culturally codified interactions that keep the illusion intact. In truth, this illusion is no less than a cosmic death wish, and it is from the illusion – this nightmare – that *Lessons Along the Way* calls us to awaken.

Storytelling at its best is an act of evolution, opening possibilities for new stories to emerge. Were *Lessons Along the Way* only about the ravages of power-over, the story would be half told. Instead, by sharing deeply from the lives of people who supported and challenged him in his own struggles, Keil illumines pathways toward a more hope-filled world, an evolving consciousness of connection.

The author delivers vital lessons about the competencies that potentiate a spirituality of authentic power. First and foremost, the reader witnesses the transformative power of empathy as daily practice. Those of us who know Richard Keil personally and readers who come to know him through this volume will quickly recognize that this daily practice is empathy with an "edge."

Most often, we think of empathy as the capacity to walk another's shoes; indeed, it is a cognitive-emotional experience that enables us to deeply resonate with the experience of another. What we see in *Lessons Along the Way* is a full blossoming of that competency and more. However, if empathy is understood to be nothing more than an "I-feel-your-pain" interaction, it might easily devolve into a tactic of ego-gratification, or worse, exploitation. Empathy, at its most radical, makes no requirement of the other. It is rooted in radical respect for what is real and present in the relationship in the moment. While it is rooted in radical acceptance, it confers neither agreement nor approval.

Although not specifically detailed in this book, my own experience of an empathic encounters with Richard Keil vividly mirror those recounted in *Lessons Along the Way*. In one instance, I expected him to indulge my often-repeated litany of the ruptures and violations I experienced during a deeply painful period in my life. In this encounter, a solicitous "I-feel-your-pain" response might have provided a temporary palliative. Instead, he pushed me to see new possibilities. In another encounter, his response to my excitement about a recent accomplishment was to remind me that any such "accomplishment" was illusory so long as it remained a distraction from my ultimate commitments.

In hurt and in happiness, his gift of empathy was a clear and compassionate version of "Take up your bed and walk!" In a very real sense, this is the empathy that compelled his encounters with Thelma, Esau, Sister Julian and Theresa, the young black girl in Alabama, helping her to envision new possibilities. It is this daring empathy that opens the portal to conflict: not conflict for conflict's sake, but to create space where bolder and more authentic truths can emerge. The empathy that we witness in *Lessons Along the Way* is the kind that shepherds, in the words of the hymnist, "beyond our wants, beyond our fears, from death to new life."

Moving from death to new life is more than a metaphor. It speaks to a consciousness that insists on believing that the world as we see it is not the world that should be or must be. As the poet Gwendolyn Brooks beautifully articulated, it consists of "not believing the details, just because we live them." There is a no more visible signifier of this kind of consciousness than the Harriet Tubman Museum that Keil founded.

Keil saw an opportunity to proclaim the struggle for human liberation and dignity. It is no accident that he chose Harriet Tubman as the guiding inspiration for his dream. She was, after all, a great shepherd who confronted the evil of slavery in a culture that based its economics, politics, and all too often religion, on the premise of white supremacy.

That the museum continues to grow and thrive is telling evidence that this consciousness is a force for good that ultimately cannot be overcome. It is a testament to the truth that neither powers nor principalities – whether they be high-ranking authorities or naysayers entrapped in illusions of the everyday world – can separate us from our calling to be one with each other.

There is a saying that I first heard attributed to an antebellum slave preacher. It is simply this: "If the Kingdom of God is within you, then everywhere you go you leave a little bit of heaven behind." Read Keil's *Lessons Along the Way*; you will experience a little bit of heaven.

Maureen Walker, PhD
Harvard University
Graduate school of Business Administration

Preface

THE MORNING SEEMED LIKE ANY other at St. Mary Catholic Church.

The same dozen or so parishioners who usually attended the 6:30 Mass were there waiting – the professor from Savannah State, the retirees, the neighbors from across the street, each silently occupying the same space on the same pew as every other weekday morning.

But I knew this Thursday was different. I knew it would be my last Mass as a priest, the last time I would proclaim the Gospel or consecrate the bread used during the Eucharist.

Whereas I normally would be praying or meditating as I waited in the sacristy for Mass to start, this day I went through a mental checklist. My letter of resignation was written and in the mail. My suitcase was packed. I would go to the bank as soon as it opened. I would call the Bishop just before hitting the road. Only then would anyone in Savannah know of my plans.

The plans were hastily constructed, but hardly rash. I had seen plenty that made me question my vocation in the 33 years since I first began training for the priesthood. Assigned to African-American parishes for the bulk of my career, I had watched many in the Church's hierarchy idly stand by as blacks struggled to overcome oppression. I had seen the Church's cruel treatment of its own, slapping down priests and nuns who disagreed with its policies, while protecting those who committed crimes against children.

It was the giving, salt-of-the-earth parishioners and the many hard-working, humble clergy that had kept the idea of leaving the priesthood on the periphery of my thoughts. That is, until my meeting with the Bishop the day before. That meeting just 12 hours earlier, on May 25, 1988, my 55th birthday, brought it to the forefront.

I'd had my disagreements with the Bishop in the past. As in any work situation, it's impossible to always see eye-to-eye. But our latest spats had been more serious. I had discussed with him concerns from parents that a fellow priest was a pedophile, but the Bishop was dismissive. We also had bumped heads over another priest who was an alcoholic and reportedly had gotten into physical fights with parishioners. The Bishop waved off that complaint as well.

On that May evening, we were discussing plans for St. Mary. The church, officially called Church of the Most Pure Heart of Mary, was in a Savannah neighborhood where drugs were rampant. Previous bishops had given up on the place, closing the school even though schools are often the community's very heart and soul at inner-city churches like St. Mary. The parish had little money, but was rich with good, earnest people.

Though I had been assigned to the church for only five months, it didn't take me long to assess the situation there: The spirit of the church was low, the finances wobbly, and no one was discussing which direction the parish should take in the future. Church members, still feeling the impact of their school closing years before, would often say they felt like orphans in the Diocese. Without a school as a focal point, they had no vision of where the parish should go. Neither did the Bishop.

The previous pastor had been diligent about pursuing potential avenues for St. Mary, with some successes and some failures. While my time there had been short, I felt I had a good plan for how to address the church's problems and lay a foundation for its future. I had spent virtually my entire career living in, working in and studying struggling parishes like this one – Southern, African-American, impoverished. This was more or less my expertise.

True, I wasn't Southern, black or poor. My childhood and teenage years had been spent in Wisconsin, followed by a stint in the Army, where I was assigned to Europe. Before moving to Alabama in 1956, most of what I knew of the Land of Cotton had come courtesy of fellow soldiers.

But I had learned much since then, from generous people who helped me to see God through the graceful way they handled adversity. All of those rich experiences that made me feel exceptionally qualified to offer a plan for the St. Mary. However, the Bishop had no intention of following any plan offered up by the likes of me.

I presented to him my ideas for the parish, the main one being consolidation. Parishioners were burdened with keeping up two city blocks of buildings that included a church, a rectory, an empty school and a vast playground. The buildings drew rampant vandalism and crime.

Weeks earlier, I had told the Bishop about a terrifying incident in which a man threw cement blocks at my bedroom window at 3 a.m. That, too, was dismissed by the Bishop with a joke. He suggested I sleep in another part of the rectory. I was accustomed to living fearlessly in the rough inner cities of America, but his mockery of my situation hurt and left me feeling angry and depressed. I had put those feelings behind me and was ready to talk about the church's future.

But the Bishop still had our previous conversations on his mind, those about the pedophilic and alcoholic priests. He was irritated with me that day and made it clear he didn't want to hear my plan. Instead, he lectured me relentlessly, suggesting that I needed counseling for depression, that perhaps this was why I had been unhappy with his decision to stand by the two priests. In fact, he told me, he would personally choose a psychiatrist for me and work with him on my treatment.

As for my feelings that St. Mary was being neglected, he boasted that he knew theology and social justice issues far better than I did and declared loudly he had God's authority and the knowledge to decide what was best for the parish, and for my life. He made it clear that I was expected to submit to his plan without question.

Case closed.

The Bishop had touched a raw nerve. The issue of my mental health had been a personal struggle for years. I tended to be overly sensitive and had battled depression since I began studying to join the Trinitarian order. I often felt I didn't measure up to the sanctity of other priests and brothers in the order. Still the patronizing situation I found myself in at that moment seemed more than I could bear.

Bruised and defeated, I returned to the rectory at Sacred Heart Church where I had been sleeping since the attempted break-in. I went to bed, but woke at 4 a.m., upset and confused. I didn't know exactly what to do, but I knew I was not going to benignly submit to the Bishop's "plan" for my life. I had tried to be obedient to the Church since beginning my journey to the priesthood in 1955. If this is where it had led me, at an impasse with a bishop unwilling to listen to me and ready to declare me mentally unstable, I knew I had to make a change.

I got my things together and drove back over to St. Mary's rectory at 4:30 a.m. In my confusion and frustration, I began to call some close friends, despite the time – Pearlie Toliver, Bobby Jones and Bill Cummings. Bill was not home, but his wife, Ann, listened to me with compassion, no doubt recalling her husband's own experience of leaving the priesthood. After I told her my story, she simply said, "Richard, get out of that place."

In those early morning hours, I made a decision that would change the course of my life: I would leave the priesthood. It would be traumatic to turn my back on the only way of life I had known, but the bravado in me said I could no longer allow others to make decisions for me, or judge what I said or did. Even if I spent the rest of my life flipping burgers or pumping gas, it would be better than this hellish existence.

At the same time, joining secular society seemed unthinkable. Since childhood, I had felt different and apart from others. I would dwell on issues few children ever think about – injustice, commitment, God. I remember mulling over these concepts at age 3 or 4. I was a kid with heightened sensitivities, too, unable to stomach people being mistreated and feeling deeply moved by people, art and music. I prayed hard each night that the world would be "right."

It was that yearning for justice that led me to the priesthood. But nothing about that Thursday morning at St. Mary seemed just. I said Mass, crying inside. I purposely distanced myself from everyone, acting as though it was just another day. When it was over, I went to the bank and cashed a check for my immediate expenses.

Driving toward the entrance for Interstate 16, I stopped at a phone booth at Shoney's and dialed the Bishop's number. The chancellor answered.

"May I speak to the Bishop? This is Richard Keil."

The chancellor, the Bishop's gatekeeper, said, "The Bishop is busy and cannot speak to you right now."

I replied, "Please tell him that I am leaving the parish and the Diocese. I have written a check and cashed it for my expenses. I am leaving."

The chancellor said, "Just a minute, Father Keil. The Bishop will speak with you."

The Bishop came on the phone.

"Bishop, I am leaving the parish and the Diocese," I told him. "I have cashed a check for my immediate expenses and I am leaving."

"Please don't leave," he said. "Just come here and we can talk."

Through tears I said, "No. I don't want to talk. I am not trying to be disrespectful to you. You always seem to out-talk me. I have just had enough. I do not wish to go through the scenario you have planned to remedy my problems. I am just tired, and I am quitting, and I do not want anyone to try to talk me out of it. I'll be in touch with you in a few days when I feel better."

The Bishop said, "Richard, do not go. ... You will be forever sorry about what you are about to do."

He offered to transfer me to another parish, to forget about making me seek mental help. But my mind was made up; I'd had enough. All the years of fighting for change, all the years of insults from Church leadership, all the years of loneliness had taken their toll.

"Thank you so much, but I just want to leave. I'm tired. I'm just leaving." I hung up and went out to my car.

The drive west to rural Twiggs County, and a little mobile home I bought while pastoring St. Peter Claver Church in nearby Macon, was long and emotional. I cried and yelled, then yelled some more. When I finally pulled up the driveway to the place that had served as my getaway, I felt a bit of peace, but was still hurting. I called a nurse I knew because I thought she would know some medicine I could take to calm down. We talked for a short time; she was stunned by my statement that I was leaving the priesthood. She said, "Get into the bathtub and take a nice, long bath."

I took my bath and began, little by little, to feel better. I called my mother, in a nursing home in Rice Lake, Wisconsin, and each of my five brothers and sisters. I wanted to be upfront with them.

"Mother, I am getting out of the priesthood. I just do not like it anymore, and I am not happy."

She did not question me or wait for a longer explanation. "Buddy, you do what makes you happy. You have been very good to so many people. Just take care of yourself. Do you need anything? I would be glad to help."

Her words were soft music to my ears. Each of my brothers and sisters said pretty much the same. None of them attend church, having left Catholicism many years before. My mother and siblings are not ones to stick their noses in another's business, but they don't hesitate to speak their minds.

I called some friends in Macon. Their support gave me the strength.

Weeks later, the Bishop and I agreed to meet at a Denny's restaurant. I waited at the front for the Bishop, reading the paper until he arrived. It was an uncomfortable situation for both of us, though he was probably more at ease given that he often met with priests under serious circumstances. He pulled out his silver cigarette holder, inserted a cigarette and lit it with a silver lighter. I hated cigarette smoke, and he never cared where he blew his.

He began, "Well, Richard, I am very sorry you are making this decision to leave. It is our policy to place a priest in your position on a one-year leave of absence. During this time, you will receive $300 a month and keep your health insurance.

"At the end of that year," he continued, "you will not receive anything from the Diocese and will not be part of our health program. When you are 65, you will receive $75 per month retirement."

I had been a priest for almost 25 years and was surprised by the paltry offering. "Are there not better benefits?" I asked.

He replied, "Our policy is the same for all priests and the Diocesan Personnel Board sets the policy. As you know, it is made up of all priests."

I was on the Board, but knew he handed down all the policies.

The Bishop continued, "The check you cashed from the parish will be deducted from your $300 per month stipend."

I knew he was giving me the velvet glove, iron fist treatment. I'm sure he thought I was being rash and immature, that I would find my way back before too long. He imagined the worst if I did not. "If you get into serious trouble, we might be able to do better," he said. "We don't want you to end up pumping gas."

I think he really did worry that pumping gas might be my fate.

"Thank you, Bishop," I said. "I appreciate your time this morning."

There I was, age 55, shaken from my comfort zone, facing decisions I had last wrestled with as a teenager deciding to join the Army and a young man deciding on the priesthood. What would the future hold? How does one go about "starting over?" The prospect was both unsettling and exciting, mostly unsettling.

I reminded myself that deciding my life course this time, as opposed to when I was much younger, was very different. This time, thankfully, I had a good sense of my place in this world. This time, I was educated, and I don't mean just in a classroom.

Sure, I had attended some fine universities, and I was grateful to the Catholic Church for that. But I also had been educated by my experiences and the good people of Russell County, Ala., and Kiln, Miss., and Macon, Ga., by cooks and laborers, by priests and nuns who endured a dysfunctional culture, survived – indeed, often thrived – and still managed to see God in everyone.

I had strategized with brave people working to change the racist America of the '50s and '60s, and met with community leaders trying to confront the oppression and challenges that remain. Many times, they had faced daunting odds. Many times, they had been forced to start over.

All of these people, all of these situations, taught me lessons – the focus of this book – that I packed up like wares and took from one city to another, one assignment to another. I was sure their words of wisdom, and the knowledge I had gained dealing with people from all walks of life, would carry me through this crisis. I would pick myself up, brush myself off. I knew the road ahead would be painful and unpredictable, but also beautiful. I would trust in God as I charted this new course, and I would listen for God's direction, as I always had.

Lessons from Early Life

CHAPTER 1

I HAVE A PRECIOUS PICTURE of my father as a young boy wearing a large white baker's hat, working in the bakery his mother opened. He quit school after second grade and each day delivered milk produced on the family farm. He was up at 4 a.m. every day, hitching up the horse and hoisting the milk bottles on the wagon, even in sub-zero Wisconsin winters. Then he'd hop into the driver's seat with his nimble 8-year-old body and take the milk to Sheboygan's front doors.

I feel pride, joy and sadness about my father, Emil Keil, working so hard, his formal education neglected, a situation that would prevent him from landing better jobs in the future. But each frosty mile he drove that milk wagon instilled in him character and strength.

My father's parents emigrated from Alsace-Lorraine, which had been passed back and forth between France and

Germany, depending on the outcome of each war. His parents were brave enough to escape that old battleground and move to the United States, to Sheboygan, in the late 1800s. Emil's mother was a resourceful woman who spoke German and broken English.

No doubt they chose Wisconsin because of the large German population there. The Germans were the dominant immigrant group in the state, but were hardly a cohesive unit. Among them were Catholics, Protestants, Jews and free-thinkers; there were craftsmen, religious refugees and farmers. They left a fragmented Germany in which culture differed from region to region.

Recently, I visited Ellis Island and I imagined my daddy as a baby in the immense, noisy halls where thousands of immigrants were processed. I imagined them as poor, frightened, tired and hungry in a strange-speaking land.

My maternal grandmother fled Ireland during the potato famine, bringing her fears and memories of British soldiers pounding down their doors in the wee hours. She died in Michigan giving birth to her fifth child, leaving my mother, Josephine Zoeller, the eldest at 16, to care for four siblings. It was an inheritance that meant hard work and poverty for many years. Her father was overwhelmed. My sister Connie once told me he was "not of much account."

I never learned much about my mother's early days. It seemed shame and guilt always surfaced and the past was not discussed. It could be that my mother was just plain tired from raising six of her own children. Such enormous responsibilities did not allow much time for talk about family history.

Much of what I know about humor and love I learned from Emil. During difficult times, my dad could tease or crack a joke. He would make toys for poorer children at Christmas. My optimism comes from him. But much of what I know about managing money comes from my mother. She also familiarized me with guilt, shame and worry.

I was born at home in 1933 during the Great Depression. My mother told me she heard the Angelus bells ringing from St. Mary's Church on that Ascension Thursday morning. I am still deciding if it was a blessing to be born on this holy day or a curse that demanded that I always remain "good."

It was a bleak time in America. The stock market crash of October 1929 left the country reeling. Factories closed and jobs evaporated. Forced to deal with this sudden, abject poverty, Wisconsin became the first in the country to create unemployment compensation.

We were as poor as everyone else. Bananas and gelatin comprised much of my early diet because I was sickly. Still my childhood was happy. I remember climbing on a chair and squealing with delight as I jumped into the arms of my sisters, Mary Jo and Connie. It is the earliest of many joyous childhood memories, though as a boy I also struggled with terrifying nightmares and remember my mother comforting me in the middle of the night, me screaming until she managed to quiet me down. After having my tonsils and adenoids removed, the nightmares went away.

Our white frame home would've been tight even for a small family using both floors, but our family of six children rented only the bottom floor, while another rented the second floor. I did not feel squeezed, however, and looked forward to Saturday night baths in the portable copper tub in the middle of the living room. We would wait for the water on the cast iron, coal stove to get hot. My mother would add the hot water to the bath and test it with her elbow.

My parents were very loving and did what they could to keep us content. It was always a cause for celebration when the circus came to Sheboygan. In earlier years, I would come running home shouting, "I saw the efenuts! I saw the efenuts!" Those were, of course, the elephants. Ringling Brothers had arrived with their circus train, parading from the rail yard to the circus grounds just outside of town. It was a glorious procession with music, elephants, real lions and tigers in cages on wheels. There were clowns, laughter and beautiful women. The wagons seemed endless.

Later in the day, my mother would let us walk to the circus grounds for the fantastic sight of the circus going up. Most fascinating was watching the tents erected. There would be teams of five black men, each with gigantic sledgehammers. One man would start pounding an iron stake into the ground, then the others would join in, hammering in succession.

It seemed miraculous how five men could make those stakes almost disappear into the ground so quickly. The black men's backs were bare and their sweaty muscles were enormous. I was amazed at their strength. It never occurred to me that I had never seen anyone else like them around Sheboygan. Later, I learned that the circus was held outside the city limits because black people were not allowed to stay overnight in the city.

Most years, my family could not afford see the actual circus. In our struggle to make ends meet, we saved money wherever we could, eschewing luxuries. We walked to school and walked home for lunch every day, a practice we followed until my last day of high school.

Sheboygan was ahead of the rest of America in 1937, as it offered two years of kindergarten with 4-year-olds in the afternoon and 5-year-olds in the morning. I was kept behind an extra half year in afternoon kindergarten because of my shyness, but spent only a half-year in morning kindergarten, passing on to first grade.

A classmate, Billy, always stopped at Abe Penn's drugstore for a chocolate ice cream cone. I would be envious as I watched him lick it.

I would ask, "Mama, may I get an ice cream cone like Billy?"

My mother would say, using my family nickname, "Buddy, we do not have three pennies to spend on ice cream cones. Daddy works hard for us, but we don't have any extra money."

I felt sorry that I had asked and ashamed that we were poor. I wish she had just said, "No, Buddy."

Sometimes mother would give us a penny and we would go down to Abe Penn's store and eye the different candies for a long time. Mr. Penn would patiently wait as we tried to choose between malt balls, orange slices and bridge mix. Then he'd weigh out the penny's worth of candy and put it in a bag.

Sheboygan was an All-American town, with a German tinge. I remember my teachers well. First grade was headed by Mrs. Gerlitz, who also taught my father. Mrs. Gerlitz could speak German. Because of this, a fourth-grader from Germany who didn't know English came to some of our first-grade classes. Someone said he was a Jew. He did look different, being so big and in first grade, but I paid no attention.

One day while skipping around the playground, I heard much shouting from the merry-go-round area and ran over toward a gathering crowd. No one was on the merry-go-round, but it was twirling very fast with kids along the sides pushing it hard. Then I saw that the new German Jewish boy was under it. Every attempt by him to crawl from underneath was rebuffed by other kids kicking at him. Others were shouting, "Go back home, Jew boy! Go back home, Jew!"

I couldn't believe the children were being so cruel. Why had they decided to turn on this boy? They didn't seem bothered by the look of sheer terror on his face. I looked around frantically. What could I do?

Then I saw Mrs. Gerlitz, with her gray hair and rimless glasses, hurrying from the school, yelling at the shouting mob of kids. She stopped the merry-go-round, picked up the larger boy and, glaring at the crowd, said, "Shame on you! You could have hurt Abraham.

"You are doing mean things, and you should be ashamed. Now go to your rooms at once. I don't want to hear one word out of anyone. Go to your rooms at once. I will see all of you later!"

I have never forgotten the cruelty of the children that day, the scared look on Abraham's face. I had stood there, completely stunned that such a thing could be happening, but hoped never to be so paralyzed and helpless again if something that dreadful was occurring.

When I was getting ready to enter the second grade, my mother said matter-of-factly of my new teacher, "Mrs. Johnson likes people who have money, and she gives those children extra help."

I was a bit apprehensive. We, of course, had no money. I worried that Mrs. Johnson would not pay attention to me. What if she talked to everyone else in the class but me? How would I learn? Could I figure out the work on my own? I had always been a child who was eager to please.

There was no need to worry. In the course of a few weeks, I found Mrs. Johnson to be wonderful and helpful, not at all what I had feared. I was pleased when she would call on me and say, "Richard, could you read the next part of our book?" Or "Richard, that was very good."

My mother didn't turn out to be right about Mrs. Johnson, but she was trying to prepare us for a sometimes cruel and unfair world, one that would equate our poverty with our worth. My parents tried to look out for us and always told us if a teacher ever hit us, we had their permission to leave.

I do not know why or how my parents came to this bold statement; they weren't confrontational with others. But I found out later that my father had been exposed to beatings, and they didn't want the same for us.

Emil's father brewed beer in tubs for the family's consumption. I don't think he sold it; it was the days of prohibition. But he drank too much of his own beer and would beat Emil. So my father never hit his own children. My mother never spoke much of her difficult childhood; I don't know if she suffered similar abuse.

In third grade, I fell in love with my teacher Mrs. Weiss. I wanted to marry her. I'll never forget the day she asked us to draw anything we wanted, something we thought was beautiful. Wisconsin has no mountains, but I drew a picture of a beautiful mountain with some clouds and a lake in front of it and smoke coming from the mountain, like a volcano. We turned in our pictures, and the next day Mrs. Weiss handed them back. That is, to everyone but me.

Then Mrs. Weiss said, "Richard, look on the board. Your picture is so pretty that I wanted all to see it."

I did not know what to do with her compliment. It felt as though my heart would burst. I have always been so proud of that moment and that picture.

Over the years, my mother saved our school report cards. They all have similar comments about me. "Richard participates well in class and is eager to answer questions and to give his comments." Once, Mrs. Weiss added an ominous note, "Richard seems to get upset when he has difficulty with something." That trait followed me the rest of my life. I am grateful that I came from a patient family.

Every evening, about 5 p.m., we ate supper together. It was not easy for the Keil children to be excused from eating with the family. My older sisters talked about boys in their school and usually made fun of them. Their conversations made me wonder: Were other girls making fun of me?

We were allowed to talk about anything we wanted at supper with a few exceptions: We could not say we didn't like school, or even hint that we didn't plan to do our best work. My dad would not tolerate such talk. Life had taught him how hard it was to live with only a second-grade education. It became clear to me that learning was important, that doing well in school was an easy way to win praise and encouragement.

I read a lot, my grades were great, and I had many friends. The world was changing very quickly. President Roosevelt had died in Warm Springs, Georgia, a place that always sounded so far away. I would come to know and love the area later in life. My mother and father admired Roosevelt for all he had done for the poor. During the bad times, my father had worked a WPA job. He was ashamed of the job, but the wages kept us fed. And my father was grateful that he worked for a living when so many could not. I wish I could take the shame from my father and thank him today for being a great man.

World War II brought rationing and a nationwide campaign for metal and steel. A souvenir World War I cannon that was in one of Sheboygan's parks was melted down for the war effort. But, at the same time, the economy picked up. My father found employment as a millwright, working at a plant making explosives near Baraboo, Wisconsin. Baraboo was 150 miles away. He would travel back to Sheboygan on occasion to see us. Gas was scarce, and we had no car, so he caught rides with other workers or took the bus home.

Then he got a job even farther away, at the atomic bomb plant in Washington state. He and the other workers did not know what they were working on. They knew it was a secret and something powerful.

My father didn't write well because of leaving school so early, but would pen letters to the family and cards to each of us children. I have dozens of cards he sent to me during the war.

> Dear Richard
> How are you I hope
> Fine and good to
> Mother …

> Well have a good
> Time my love to you
> Daddy

It was hard living without him, but we all pitched in to help my mother. The time seemed to drag on forever. But finally the war ended. Germany surrendered in May 1945. Four months later, Japan followed suit.

Celebrations broke out across the United States. Ticker tape rained down; perfect strangers kissed in the streets. The world was suddenly a joyous place. The good guys had won.

My dad came home and was offered a carpenters' union job in Racine – for a whole dollar an hour. The end of the war brought an exciting new beginning for the Keils. We were moving from Sheboygan to Racine.

CHAPTER 2

THE CHILDREN MADE FUN OF Mr. Ritter, the short, bald-headed principal with the squeaky voice. They made fun of Mrs. Ford, the older history teacher whose saggy stockings always gathered around her ankles. They made fun of Mr. Merman, calling him "Fatty Merman."

Racine, in many ways, was very different from Sheboygan. I had never before heard children ridiculing teachers.

Everything seemed a bit more city-like here, 85 miles to the south. The neighborhoods were bustling. Some had their own grocery store, drug store, butcher and bakery. Downtown was full of shops. The city was rich with theaters, the Rialto, the Venetian, the Capitol, the Crown, Main Street, Douglas Avenue. Dances were held at the recreation center on Friday nights; bands played in the zoo on Sundays. We celebrated the Fourth of July with decorated doll buggy parades in the public parks and a bigger procession downtown, with floats and marching bands like the Boys of '76.

Here, I began to change, ever so slightly. I began to run with a rougher crowd, one not so interested in good grades and learning. I still did well in school and didn't dare talk badly about the teachers. After all, while this may have been a new city, I still had the same parents. But eventually I found myself studying just enough to get by. Adolescent cynicism began to rub off onto me.

Not all of the teachers were targeted by the students. Even the delinquents knew how far was too far. No one – and I mean no one – made fun of Mrs. Becker, the math teacher. She made everyone sit with legs exactly in front of his or her desk and allowed no slouching in the seats. If a student came up to her immaculate desk and put his hands on it, she would gently open her top drawer, pull out a cloth and ask him to remove the fingerprints.

Her 5-foot frame and 90-pound body cast an imposing presence. Sometimes, high school students who were behind in their studies would be sent back to the Junior High for periods of time. They would be assigned temporarily to Mrs. Becker's room because she could control them with little trouble. These older and bigger students cared nothing for school or conformity – but even they knew Mrs. Becker was the boss.

Then there was Ray Kayon – "Big Ray," but only in whispers, never when he had even the itsiest possibility of hearing it. Mr. Kayon was my homeroom teacher. He was tall and handsome. He served during WWII, finished his studies and played football at the University of Wisconsin. In homeroom, he would challenge us to act like gentlemen. If the class was misbehaving, or talking badly about a girl, he would stop and chew us out. "You wimps think you are so damn smart and tough, but you are weak for treating girls badly. Be a damn man and don't be harsh to girls." Sometimes he would say to me, "Keil, you are a gentleman, and I want you to stay that way. Don't be led by some of these other punks."

When junior high football started up for the first time ever, and Mr. Kayon posted the varsity lineup, I was named a starting running back. I was only 110 pounds in ninth grade. After being a sickly child, eating bananas and gelatin and having nightmares, I could hardly believe I would be running back. But I had committed myself to trying all sports since an incident years earlier, back in Sheboygan.

A classmate, Bob Farhes, and I were best friends until we got into an argument. His father was down in Alabama, a captain in the Army. He made good money for the times, and Bob always seemed to have everything he wanted. He was a large, brown-headed guy, and seemingly gentle and honest.

Then, one day Bob said, "Dick, I took some money from my mom's purse. Do you want to go Penn's drug store and get some candy?"

It freaked me out to think he had stolen from his mother. "No, Bob, your mother might find out and tell my momma."

All of a sudden I was on the ground and he was pinning me down.

"Dick, promise me you won't tell your mom. Promise me, promise me!"

I could not escape. He held my head down in the snow. I was hardly able to breath. I was surprised, frightened and angry but could do nothing. He didn't care and continued to shove my face into the snow. Finally, he let me up and went home. We remained friends, but I distanced myself. Probably as much as anything, this spurred my interest in boxing, wrestling and other sports that required defending oneself.

It helped that Mr. Kayon was always encouraging. He was a strong man, but not a bully. Most of the boys and girls admired him, even when he corrected us. I counted myself lucky to have been assigned him as a teacher as I worked to adapt to a new city and new environment. Mr. Kayon was an honorable man, and he pushed us Junior High boys to be the same.

When I moved on to high school, I rarely saw Mr. Kayon. I think he continued coaching and maybe became an assistant superintendent of schools. I was always thankful that he had shown such confidence in me, even though I wasn't the most vocal or the most assertive.

In high school, I joined the Catholic Youth Organization. I had been going to church on Sundays and attended more often during Lent. I would get up very early, get dressed, make a sandwich and walk ten blocks to 5:30 a.m. Mass at St. Edward Church. After Mass, I would eat, then walk another 10 blocks to school. I did not discuss this with my parents or anyone else. I just did it on my own.

In time, I was elected president of the CYO, which seemed very unusual. I went to public school, and most of the students at CYO were from the parochial St. Catherine's High School. I was jealous because I knew it cost a lot of money to go there. At first, the kids seemed cliquish, but they accepted me.

Washington Park High School was mostly uninspiring, except for Mrs. Gordon, the pretty new science teacher and girls' gym teacher.

"Richard, I will not accept this science paper from you. You are capable of good things in science. Do it over."

"Richard, I read the paper you re-did. It is an excellent treatment of osmosis."

"Richard, I want you to come to the girls' gym during your study hall hour. Your work is going down, and I will not accept it. We need to talk."

I liked Mrs. Gordon because she made me toe the line. She demanded that I put in the effort and turn in the kind of work she knew I was capable of producing. She was always determined. Some thought her mean. But she expected much from us – especially me.

It was difficult to concentrate on school, at times. The Korean War was raging, and I expected to go and fight. The boys in school would say to each other, "Heck, no use trying hard in class just to go and get my behind shot off in Korea."

Like many of them, I didn't have money to go to college. College was not for me, I thought. For lower income kids who survived Korea, the factory was the next destination. My parents, dear and loving as they were, knew little of higher education. Their general expectations were for me to be good, work hard, support myself and maybe get married. Their modest backgrounds, the struggles of their upbringings, the humbling times of the Depression and two world wars had left them with a limited outlook.

I dated several girls in school. Being shy, I was normally asked out by the girls. Since I had no money, I felt inferior and unattractive. It was thanks to the goodness and boldness of Karen Farenback that I went on my first date. I barely had enough money to take her to a 12-cent movie. I was warned by girls in my class not to go with her. They said she was not so nice. Little did I know the girls in my class were jealous of her beauty and intelligence. We had a good time on our date, and she was wonderful. Some years later in the seminary, I found out that her sister became Miss Wisconsin in the Miss America pageant. We liked one another but never went out again. I never asked her, mostly because I was ashamed of being poor.

I had a crush on Mary Lou Chausky, a pretty blonde cheerleader. We never dated but we laughed the whole semester in printing, typing and driving classes.

Ronald Jander and I were best friends. Ron was a star in football and basketball. His mother died early. And, while he had a good father, Ron began to raise himself. Chasing girls and drinking were his main interests. He would always tell me, "Rich, you're a great guy," and confide in me his deepest secrets. We would go to the dances at Devine's Million Dollar Ballroom in Milwaukee. There, we would hear big bands like Tommy and Jimmy Dorsey, Louis Armstrong, Duke Ellington, Gene Krupa and Woody Herman.

Ron's good looks, friendliness, athletic prowess and lack of interest in his studies may have been why he was voted president of our graduating class. Later, I was the best man at his wedding.

Jack Bryant was the vice president of the Class of 1951. Before, in Sheboygan, I had never attended school with a black person. Jack and I played football and wrestled together. We were both small and competitive. We were friendly toward one another, but it wasn't until we worked together the first summer after high school that we became friends.

It was in my final year of high school that I decided to quit sports and get an afternoon job. In previous years, I had caddied during the summer. Then I was the popcorn boy at the Capitol Theatre, which had been built in the 1920s and had beautiful, ornate plasterwork and stenciling. I wanted a better job. I went to a shopping center and began to go from store to store, asking if anyone needed help. After several trips, I came across Midwest Tire and Auto, and the manager agreed to see me.

"Hey, I'm Irv Schuman. How can I help you?" said a large man with a large mustache.

"I'm Richard Keil, and I'm looking for a part-time job. I'm a hard worker, willing to learn."

"Well, we don't need anyone. But, if you give me your phone number, I'll call you if something comes up."

I gave him my name and phone number, and continued my inquiries. After a few more stores, and more rejections, I started walking home, resigned to the idea that I would continue to work as a popcorn boy at the Capitol Theatre.

Sometime after arriving home, the phone rang. My mother answered. "You wish to speak to Richard Keil? Yes, he's right here."

"This is Irv Shulman, the manager of Midwest Tire and Auto Stores. We talked earlier today; you said that you were looking for a part-time job. If you want to work, come here tomorrow at 7:30. We will pay you 10 dollars a week, and you will be our seat cover boy and put in batteries."

I was thrilled. I knew nothing about cars or repairs. He didn't ask, and I didn't tell.

I learned fast. I'd pull out the seats of each car, carrying them up a couple flights of stairs, put the seat covers on, carry the seats back down and reinstall them within an hour.

At the end of the first week, Irv came to me and said, "Here is $15. You did a good job, and we will pay you $15 next week."

I was ecstatic.

As time went on, I learned more. Batteries, shock absorbers, tires, brakes, wheel bearings, gaskets, universal joints, carburetors, water pumps, with more new words being added to my vocabulary. I learned who made them, where they went and the correct sizes for each car. I could not install any of these parts, but that was not my job. Little by little, my manager asked me to wait on customers. When I finished high school, Irv told me that Max and Nort Shapiro, the two owners of Midwest Tire and Auto stores, wanted to see me.

"Buddy, we are very pleased with your work, and we know that you want to work for a successful future. You could do very well with us. We want you to be a salesman and then go higher in the company. We will pay you $40 per week, from 7:30 a.m. to 6:30 p.m., six days a week."

I thought it over and decided to do it. I would not have to depend on manual labor as my father did. This rich Jewish family was taking me under its wing and was willing to teach me some very useful skills.

"Buddy, I go to Chicago every Tuesday," Nort said one day. "I go to all of our manufacturers and wholesale outlets.

Tuesday is your day off. If you want, you could come with me and learn the business inside and out."

This was an unprecedented opportunity. So each Tuesday, I went with Nort to Chicago. Nort, his brother and two nephews owned a dozen stores and wanted more.

Nort asked, "Buddy, would you consider taking the electric train to Milwaukee each day and become our assistant manager at our store at 805 Mitchell Street? We will pay your expenses and increase your salary – $40 per week, plus 1 percent of the gross sales of the store."

This was wonderful. I was 18 years old and doing so well.

Jack found out I was working at Midwest Tire and Auto and called and asked if I could get him a job. My boss hired him, and we quickly became friends.

Some months later, I got a frantic call from my oldest sister, Mary Jo. "Buddy, could you help me? Vic is hurting me, and I have to leave town. He wants to kill me." Vic was her husband, a well-known attorney in Racine.

"Where do you want to go, Mary? I'll come get you."

"Take me to the bus station in Milwaukee, and I will be all right."

I had the use of our family car, a 1948 Ford, at night; my dad drove it during the day while I either walked or took the electric train to work. I thought I might need help if Mary Jo's husband was hostile, so I asked Jack to go with me. He was happy to help. We drove my sister to Milwaukee, and she never went back to her husband. That night really solidified my friendship with Jack. He was the first black person I'd ever gotten to know. For the most part, he was just like me. I was glad I had helped him get the job at Midwest.

Some months later, the manager of the Mitchell Street store ran off with a woman, and I got another call.

"Buddy, this is Nort. We would like you to be manager of the Mitchell Street store. Yes, we know that you are 18 and the other five salesmen are married and older, but we think you can do the job. We will pay you $50 a week and 2 percent of the gross sales."

It was good money, I thought. I would be able to help my parents and save. I had begun paying my mother and father for room and board as soon as I left high school. They never asked me for a dime, but I loved them and had learned good money management skills from my mother. The manager's job sounded like the right move.

Uncle Sam had other thoughts.

I received notice from the draft board that my name would come up sometime in the next year, and I would be drafted for service in Korea. It was a sobering thought. One minute, I was looking forward to my new job as manager of the tire shop; the next, I was waiting to go overseas. I had always considered myself patriotic and willing to do what my country asked of me. So, instead of waiting around to be drafted, I decided to volunteer. I wanted to get it over with so I could get on with my life.

After saying goodbye to the Shapiros, who had taught me so much and showed such great confidence in me, I said a tearful goodbye to my mother and father. My sister, Joyce, came to see me off from Fort Sheridan, Illinois. There, I saw a friend from high school, Bob Olson, who was accompanied by his girl, Marjorie Frost. We were headed to Fort Ord, California. The war was on, and combat awaited us. We were scared as hell, but we did not blink.

CHAPTER 3

THE RECRUIT STAMMERED AND HESITATED, and that was enough to set off the impatient sergeant.

This one, the sergeant decided, he'd make an example of, in case any of the rest of us even thought about procrastinating when he gave an order. It would be my first time witnessing barracks humor.

"Private, you and me are going to sick call tomorrow," the sergeant said.

The recruit responded in an innocent and puzzled manner. "Why do we have to go to sick call together?"

"So we can have my foot removed from your ass!" the sergeant responded.

All of us laughed. But I couldn't stop laughing. The sergeant looked at me. "Private, get down and give me 30 push-ups."

Smiling, I did what I was told, saying to myself, hell, I can do as many of these as he wants. And there you have Basic Training – bravado ruled the day.

In Basic Training, I encountered all types: blacks, Latinos, rich, poor, Muslims, Jews, educated and barely literate. In 1948, President Truman had issued an executive order prohibiting segregation in the armed forces. If there were soldiers who had a problem with this, they kept it to themselves while the Sarge was around. Basic training was learning how to survive, learning how to kill. The killing part gave me pause. I understood that killing is a part of war. Still it felt wrong, as we were training, to hear so many soldiers shouting, "Kill those goddamn yellow Korean gooks!" as a way to pump themselves up.

One day, while we were lined up in formation, a couple of recruits protested, saying they would not kill. I could not believe it. In front of the whole company of soldiers, these two guys quietly said that they were conscientious objectors. The officers, the sergeants and the troops went crazy, vehemently denouncing them. The two recruits were arrested and put in the brig. I thought the men a bit strange and a bit weak. But, for the first time, I realized that there were people willing to take a stand against killing, even during war time.

Though I first thought of the conscientious objectors as mere sissies, they set off a thought process for me that I had never explored really. I did not want to be a conscientious objector. I would fight for the United States and do what was asked for these two years that I was in the Army. But, at the same time, I wondered how that fighting would affect the rest of my life.

I did not believe that we should kill people because they were yellow, and I did not think that some people were gooks. What's more, I did not believe that we should lock up conscientious objectors.

I began to think and read. I told no one of my thoughts. I just continued trying to be a good soldier. Several times, I was named Soldier of the Day. But, more and more, I pondered right and wrong and the best way to spend the rest of my life if I wanted to help people, not hurt them.

Maybe, I thought, I could become a doctor. No, people still die, I told myself. Maybe I could be a lawyer. No, people still go to jail. Maybe I could be a priest. Yes, I started to think, that's a good idea. I would help people in the ultimate way, all the way to heaven.

Was I priest-like? I surely wasn't like any of the priests I knew. I had always been a Catholic, but I had never even been to a Catholic school. I knew nothing of the inner workings of the Church and the priesthood. Still, the idea appealed to me.

Basic training ended followed by advanced infantry training, which was followed by three weeks of special combat training. We were now mentally and physically tough. We were ready to go to Korea.

We knew there would be orders to go to Camp Stoneman in Pittsburg, California, then to ship out to Korea. It wasn't a pleasant thought, but it was reality.

Then, in 1953, an armistice was signed. Great! I rejoiced. We would go to Korea, but not to get killed.

Our duty orders were read over the P.A. system: "Private Jones, FECOM," meaning, the Far East Command, Korea. "Private Olson, FECOM. Private Smith, FECOM. Private Keil, EUCOM," meaning European Command. Six of the 300 men were going to Europe. The rest were going to Korea. Only God and the Army could figure it out.

It was exciting – I would be going to Europe and visiting my mother and father on the way. In an instant, life had turned beautiful.

From Fort Ord, I flew United Airlines to Chicago, then got the train to Racine. I was so proud and happy. Then it was off to Camp Kilmer, N.J., where I waited to ship off to Germany.

I pulled kitchen duty at Camp Kilmer and was assigned to be the bartender at the Officers' Club. A few days before, officers were yelling at us at Fort Ord, and now I was listening to their tales of woe over beer. It was my first counseling job.

My first cruise also came courtesy of the Army. In the deep bowels of the USNS General Maurice Rose, our canvas bunks were stacked four high and close together, allowing mere inches between one body and another. The ship swayed in rough storms and the seasick men above sometimes vomited on those in the bottom bunks.

As large as our ship was, with its thousands of GIs, it was tossed around like a cork. The propeller would come out of the water as the front part of the ship went down. Never had I seen such massive power at sea. I loved it.

A Latino fellow began to talk with me as we were standing on the upper deck watching the thunderous waves. "Hey, I'm Pedro. What's your name?" He had a large mustache and longish sideburns.

"I'm Richard. Where ya from?"

"I'm from Texas," he replied. "There are a lot of guys from Texas here."

We were alone, and we talked easily for a long time.

A little later, when the thousands of guys were lining up to eat lunch, I noticed across the room that my new friend Pedro was in the middle of a bunch of guys. They all seemed to be Latino. Then some Anglos came by. There was a flurry of words and a little shoving on this overcrowded ship in the middle of the Atlantic. All of a sudden, the place quieted down. Pedro said a few words, put a knife back in his pocket and peace seemed to resume. I didn't know what had happened, but Pedro was surely the leader of the troops, even though he was a private just like me. It was amazing to see his natural leadership.

A few days later, I saw Pedro and a few of his friends crudely clowning around. They would wait until the mess line was quite long. They knew some of the men were seasick and the smell of food wasn't making things better. Pedro and a couple of his friends would feign sickness and run over to the garbage cans and pretend they were vomiting. Then they would rise from their stance and begin to laugh. The whole mess hall would crack up. It was the entertainment for several thousand soldiers packed like sardines on a ship for a week. I thought it was hilarious like everyone else, except the sick guys.

There were duty assignments on the ship, but when I reported to my duty station, the sergeant told me they had enough help. I was free the whole trip to talk, play cards, look at the sea and its huge, violent waves. I spent much time thinking and reading.

We landed in Bremerhaven, Germany, and the first astonishing thing I saw were the German workers with their used paint cans dipping into our garbage cans to try to grab food for themselves and their families. I had never seen anything like that. Being a northern seaport, the city was almost completely destroyed during WWII bombings. We were ordered off the ship and immediately put on troop trains heading for Zweibrucken, a receiving and assignment center for the U.S. Army forces in Europe. All of this travel was exhilarating for me after the rigors of 20 weeks of infantry training.

The train ride was interesting and awakening. There were women in the fields behind horse-pulled plows. The aftermath of World War II was still very visible. The German train crewmembers were nice, and the bunks were clean and comfortable. I, of course, had never encountered so many different types of people. It was a great opportunity, even if I didn't know what tomorrow held or where I would be assigned. I presumed I would carry a rifle for a couple of years and live in the fields of Germany.

The Zweibrucken receiving base was orderly and large, able to accommodate huge populations for a short time before assigning the troops all over Europe. No longer was there the harsh treatment of Basic Training. People were clear and civil in giving orders or directions. This was a welcomed relief.

The next day found me in a long line in a large building. We waited until one of the Army assignment personnel was free to see us. There were literally dozens and dozens of desks with these personnel, each one ready to interview a new soldier.

So many of the men had told me they were going to try to get out of the infantry by asking for some specialized Army school or asking to be a chaplain's assistant or whatever it took. I said nothing. I thought I would take whatever came to me.

To my surprise, when my turn for assignment came up, I saw that the person I was talking to was a private. He seemed comfortable and confident, but I was surprised that a mere PFC could have any power to send anyone anywhere. We greeted one another, and he asked me if I had any idea what the Army might hold for me. I told him that I would do whatever the Army asked of me. Then he surprised me.

He said, "I see that you have worked with auto parts and had typing in high school. Would you like to go to England and work as a motor pool parts clerk?"

I said, "What is that? It sounds interesting."

He said, pointing a finger to a corner, "Go over to that desk and take the typing test."

In about 10 minutes, I brought the test back for him to see. I had passed it.

"Good," he said. "I'm going to try to assign you to England. You will not be in the infantry but in the ordnance part of the army assigned to a motor pool. Would you like that?"

I was a new private, but common sense told me this ordinary PFC was about to instantly change my life for the better. I would no longer be possible cannon fodder as an infantry private, but rather have a job with auto parts, an area where I had real expertise.

"You will be hearing something in a few days," the PFC assured. "This may not go through, so don't get your hopes up too high. This is still the Army and things get screwed up."

I said, "Thanks so much for your help. It's nice to meet you."

"I hope it works out," he said.

Later, we were all gathered in a large auditorium. We were being told how to act overseas and how to avoid venereal diseases. "We will court-martial your ass if you catch VD. You got that, soldiers? You better get it, damn you."

Suddenly, I heard the large overhead speaker announce, "Private Keil, report to the rear of the building. Major Barfield is there to see you."

My heart jumped. In front of these thousands of GIs, I got up, wondering what I may have done wrong. I began the long walk to the back of the cavernous auditorium. The major was at the back door.

"Keil?"

"Yes, sir."

"Come outside. I have some orders for you."

This was too good to be true, I thought. I felt like a millionaire on vacation traveling to these countries. The major and I exchanged a few cordial words as he took me to the station. Looking back, it seemed to be an act of God.

Once on the train and speeding to the Hook of Holland, I went to the dining car and there on the German menu were the words "wiener schnitzel." I didn't know what it was, but I had heard of it so I ordered it. With the little German I knew and the little English of the waiter, I was served well.

I made up my mind I would always be a courteous American soldier overseas. Something was changing in me as I experienced new countries and different people. I had time to think and reflect.

The train completed its journey to the North Sea, and I boarded the ferry going to England. I was assigned to a stateroom with my own bed and bathroom. The dining rooms were shown to me, and the crew spoke English very well. I went off to sleep in my soft bed, rocking to the rhythm of the sea. The next morning, the ferry reached England.

Besides the U.S. Army, no one in the world knew where I was. There had been no time to write my family. I got on the train to Liverpool Station and went to the dining car for breakfast. I ordered tea and the waitress poured cream into it. I put some sugar into it and was surprised at how much I liked it. From then until I left England, I happily acclimated myself to their tea and gave up coffee.

There was a soldier waiting to pick me up at the station. We got into an Army truck and went through London to a nearby U.S. Army base. It was the headquarters of the Army in England. I stayed a couple of days, then boarded a train to Bicester. There, I was picked up by another soldier and taken to the Company Commander of Upper Heyford, 4th Artillery Battalion to be an assistant parts clerk of the motor pool.

I reported to the Commander's Office, and he had a clerk show me my bunk and locker in the barracks. The barracks were metal Quonset huts, my home for two years. For 24 guys, this would be the setting where we would get to know each other, encourage each other, make fun of each other, fight, struggle, and sometimes learn to hate each other. At times, it got ugly. When Jack Strong was especially drunk, he would take his trenching shovel and try to kill whomever he could reach. We would subdue him and tie him to his bed. If we were to get any sleep and avoid a beheading, it seemed the only solution.

There were constant insults and barbs about the black soldiers among the white soldiers. There were insults and barbs about the white soldiers among the black soldiers. I tried to be friends with everyone. But some of the guys, black and white, I could take or leave.

Joe Steele was a husky, blond loudmouth from one of the Carolinas. In the barracks, in the mess hall, in the beer joint, he spewed his so-called knowledge and bragged about his alleged conquests. Sex – how much he was getting, where he planned to get it next – was his favorite topic. And when he had talked that to death, he and his buddies moved on to blacks: how lazy they were, how nasty they were, how dumb they were, how immoral they were.

I tried to ignore him as much as possible, but couldn't help wondering how many others in the South were that racist and crass. Because of my job as clerk of the motor pool, I was on good terms with almost everyone. Soldiers needed parts for their trucks, and I was the guy who could get them. It was easy work and my officers appreciated me, giving me letters of commendation and bottles of whiskey as presents. Their letters made me feel proud. The whiskey made friends, because I gave it away.

I liked to go to the beer bar on base just to talk with the guys. On occasion, I would go to nearby Oxford to the pubs and restaurants. I began to read John Henry Newman's *Apologia Pro Vita Sua*. It was the first book that I read as I began to explore the possibility of the priesthood. I still told no one, and no one made fun of me for reading such a heavy book. Most probably did not know or care about the book.

Everyone talked about going to London. This was postwar England and Britain was poor and recovering from the war. Yankee soldiers had money and spent it like water. I managed my money well. I had $37.50 taken from my monthly $82 pay put into U.S. Savings Bonds. I even took that same amount from my $78 pay in basic training.

Guys were always talking of places where they could get drunk, pick up women and stay the weekend. I wanted to go to London. It would be wonderful if I met a great woman that I could share the weekend with. However, I wanted to see London. I wanted to see the museums. I wanted to see the buildings and meet the people and see movies and plays and maybe go to live music.

I was 19. I came from humble people. I liked drinking a couple of beers and maybe Scotch. I wanted to go to London and see it, not get silly-ass drunk. I wanted to meet a lady, but I wanted her to be a lady, and I wanted to be a gentleman.

So off to London I went. I saw "The Music Man" one night. It was so funny. Since it was about America, I felt a little at home. Then, near Christmas, I was feeling lonely without my family and I happened near Royal Festival Hall. There was a glorious Christmas concert there by a boys' chorus with an orchestra. I was drowned in this beautiful, loving music.

Each Sunday morning, I would get up and find a Catholic Church. London on Sunday mornings was quiet – not too many people went to church. The churches were small and poor, but going deeply satisfied something in me.

The restaurants were unpretentious. I am sure that there were fancier ones, but I did not have the knowledge or the money to splurge. I went to the British Museum with its long halls and galleries of artifacts, most of which I did not have the background to fully enjoy. But I enjoyed it in my 19-, 20-year-old manner. I visited the tomb of Cardinal John Henry Newman after I finished his book and the reply to his book, written by the Anglican Kingsley. I was beginning to learn on my own.

One night, I met a nice English man, and he invited me to go with him to a pub. Here, young students from the Middle East, Africa, France and Spain and many of the other European countries came, listened to great jazz or music from their own countries. The pub was downtown, but I was the only American there. People were good to me, but not deferential. The students were sons and daughters of the wealthy of their countries.

I began to get together with them on occasion. We would sometimes go to one of their homes after the pub closed and listen to drum music from Africa or jazz or Indian music. I met a woman, Terry. We became beloved friends for the time I spent in England. We visited museums, went to plays, movies, ate in quiet restaurants, with her introducing me to different cuisine. We also read books and did a lot of kissing, but nothing more. She set good boundaries.

One night, a prostitute visited our barracks on base. The actions of other men were so spontaneous that it was all nearly over before I realized what was happening. In the far corner of the room, I heard a commotion. I saw people looking for money in their wallets or borrowing money from others. I heard a shout, "Hey, let's get it on with her. Get in line."

One guy after another visited the end bunk to have sex. I noticed Monroe, standing by, looking uncomfortable. We looked at one another. Monroe motioned for me to come over to his bunk.

Monroe said, "Hey, Keil. Let's go to the beer bar. I got a girlfriend back in Mississippi, and I don't want any part of that."

"Monroe, that's a great idea. Let's go."

Monroe and I put on our coats and walked over to the taxi stand to get a ride to the bar. After we arrived, we talked a long time. Here was this black man from Mississippi and myself. Neither of us were saints, but we just viewed the activity in the barracks with revulsion. Never again would I listen to the racist clichés about the immorality of black men.

Army life taught me many lessons and gave me many opportunities. Being overseas, I was away from my family and friends. If I wanted to shame myself by drinking too much, no one would know. But I didn't want to. I saw First Sergeant Dozier and Sergeant First Class Ross demoted because of their drinking. I saw our company commander, Captain Smith, demoted to a corporal because of his drinking. Even though I did not drink a lot, I stopped drinking altogether for a little while. I saw guys waste their money gambling then walk around broke all month. If I wanted to run around with the wrong woman, no one would know. I didn't want to. I saw guys end up with venereal diseases.

My sergeant spent every night with a woman in Upper Heyford, never sleeping in the barracks. I was surprised when he told me that he had a wife and six children in the states.

The sergeant and I got along well, even though I couldn't respect the way he was treating his wife and family. I was amazed when he told me that he did not know how to read, write or do simple math.

"Keil," he said to me one day, "the Army is phasing out all of us older sergeants who can't read and write. Would you teach me math and how to write?" I could hardly believe what he was asking me. I had no college education.

"Yeah, Sarge," I said. "I'll be glad to try if you have the books."

For about a year, we met a couple of times a week, and he learned with the help of the books. I would like to take credit for his learning, but I was just an encouragement to him.

Captain Cory was announced as the next head of the motor pool and my new boss. He had a reputation of being tough, no nonsense. While he was an officer and I was a private, we had respect for each other. He praised me a lot and put a permanent letter of commendation in my file. I was made a corporal. This may sound like bragging, but I looked at myself as little Buddy Keil from Sheboygan, and here I was teaching my sergeant and being praised by my commanding officer. It was all so new.

I swore a lot and had sexual fantasies. I sometimes listened to racist or ethnic jokes. I foolishly made fun of some guys from Kentucky and Tennessee who played country music on their guitars, not knowing enough to appreciate their artistry. There was so much I did not know, but I was learning. I wrote my parents once a week and, with great joy, received letters from my mother. Being overseas, I was growing apart from my family in terms of likes and goals, but I don't think I was conscious of it at the time.

I never talked about my possible plans of studying for the priesthood, though I went to Mass each Sunday. I saw a notice one Sunday on the church bulletin board: "Come spend the day at Prinknash Abbey on retreat. This is a Cistercian Monastery, commonly known as Trappist monks. Lunch will be served and talks will be given by the abbot."

I thought it might be a good chance to learn about the Church.

A small group of us soldiers took a van to the Abbey. We drove through the beautiful British countryside with the stone-and-hedge fences keeping the sheep in place. We pulled up the driveway of this very old monastery. Monks with their white and black robes greeted us. We had an introduction to their way of life. No talking. No meat. Rise to pray at 3:30 a.m. No heat.

Each monk has his own knife, fork and spoon, which stayed at the monk's place in the dining room with no washing. The utensils were wrapped in napkins, which were changed each week. No communication with families and friends. No going home for funerals or burials. When the monks died, their bodies were wrapped in cloth and lowered into the ground, sans coffin.

We went to several talks given by a profoundly intellectual abbot. I had no idea what he was talking about. Neither did anyone else. For lunch, we were hungry, but they served little – their homemade bread and jams, which we devoured. We listened to more talks about God, our salvation and other spiritual mysteries.

As we left, we all agreed that we were amazed by the old monastery and the monks, but it was all a little too much for us. Little did I know that the famous Trappist monk Bede Griffith, author of the book "The Golden Thread," was a monk in the abbey. He may have been the monk talking to us. Years later, I read his book.

My time in the Army was coming to an end. I looked forward to getting out of the service. I had been on leave in Germany, France and Italy, getting free military "hops" around Europe. I had a good work experience in Upper Heyford and made a number of Army buddies. I had great British friends. Still I wanted to get on with my life.

Terry and I painfully and tearfully departed. I loved my time in England, and it helped me prepare myself to freely follow what was in my heart. I found out I didn't need to be a part of the pack. I loved the arts and meeting people from other countries. I didn't consider myself pious or better than anyone else, but I didn't want to be drunk and loosely jump into bed with women as a way of life. I wanted to go to school and become something.

Waiting for our ship to leave the dock in Southampton was boring, but I passed the time drinking more than I should have at the NCO club, making fun of the Army and laughing with other happy guys coming back home. I was no longer a private, E-1, but now a corporal, E-5.

The ship voyage home was uneventful. The seas were quieter than they were on the trip over, and the troops aboard the ship were now veterans, not recruits. As we pulled out of the Southampton Harbor, we noticed a gigantic ship docked next to ours. It must have been the Queen Mary or Queen Elizabeth. We thought that our USS Maurice Rose was a large ship, but it seemed like a rowboat next to this majestic ship. Docking in New York, we boarded a train to Fort Sheridan in Illinois.

We were processed out of the Army, received a good bit of discharge pay in cash and walked out the front gate of Fort Sheridan. Strangely, I felt out of sorts, leaving the Army with its barren familiarity.

I knew I was going to have to make important decisions about the priesthood. Did I have a calling? I had a real love for God, but how could I know if this was some heavenly invitation to lead? I certainly didn't have all the answers. Hell, I certainly hadn't even asked all the questions.

In books, some have written that those with a calling have this strong, deep feeling inside that it's God's will that they serve. No matter hard the person tries to push it aside, it persists. I considered, as best I could from the perspective of an inexperienced 21-year-old, what I would be giving up – a wife, a family, independence, money. Still the idea of the priesthood persisted. Everything about it seemed right. I considered myself compassionate, approachable and empathetic. I was a good listener and had a keen sense of justice. I wanted to serve the poor and the needy, to never again stand by as the new, Jewish kid cowered under the merry-go-round.

First, I would need to find a seminary and college that would accept me. I had only my shaky confidence, my dedication and my resolve to work hard. I would begin the journey with one step. I would find someone who could advise me.

Lessons from the Seminary

CHAPTER 4

My father didn't say much.

Most of the four-hour drive was spent in silence, with occasional comments on the scenery and intermittent reminders from my mother: Make sure to write. Try to get enough to eat. Mind the weather; Dubuque is as cold as Racine.

He had on his only suit, a brown one, and wore a dark tie with his Elks gold chain and pin. It must have been hard for my father to soak it all in. But he was a gentle man, not one to press too hard for answers. Mostly, he wanted my happiness.

"Buddy, I'm proud of you," he said. "You'll do good. If you don't like it, come home."

It was only 200 miles away. But the future that awaited – college and studies, the priesthood and vows – seemed a different world altogether. I had sought it out, but had no concept of it, other than what I saw for 90 minutes on Sundays.

Leaving for the Army had been so much different. My thoughts then centered on survival and doing right by my country. All of us headed to Basic Training were in the same situation. We were all scared, and no one knew exactly what awaited us. We assumed we would be sent to Korea, where we would do our part in the stand against communism. And, if we died, we died. Wisconsin boys answered the call.

But even that departure, just two years ago, didn't seem as uncertain as this one. And I was only going to Iowa, to Loras College, where I would start my quest to become a priest.

My mother had packed a lunch, so we stopped along the way at a roadside picnic table. The meal was nice, but seemed tinged with finality.

"Do you have enough money?" my mother asked. "Please write us each week and tell us how you are doing."

I had enough money. I took after my mother – I had been a good saver my whole life. I also was eligible for $900 per year from the GI Bill. Money, in that moment, was the least of my worries. The questions racing through my mind were of another nature. Would I be smart enough? I hadn't studied in years, and my high school study habits were lax. Will they think I'm stupid? How do I talk to the priests? What do I say to the other guys? What if they find out that I like women? Would I fit in? I didn't know much about the Church or even how to say the rosary.

Though my mother and father were Catholic, they had not been to church since the Depression. A priest had asked them to take my older sister out of Catholic school when they couldn't afford tuition. My dad did not complain, but he stopped going to church. When I told them of my decision to join the priesthood, they told me to do what was best for me; they would be happy as long as I was happy. Of course, like me, they had no idea what was involved.

The idea of pursuing a profession with a long educational preparation was not part of my family's culture. While all of us six children had been raised Catholic, none of my brothers or sisters still went to church. They never really liked it. Though my siblings didn't try to discourage me, I could tell they thought I didn't really know what I was getting myself into. And, for the most part, I didn't. I loved God and wanted to serve people. What role a church hierarchy might play in the life of a priest never crossed my mind. I assumed all those teaching and leading seminarians would be loving and supportive, just as most of the people in my life had been when I told them of my decision.

My bosses at Midwest Tire and Auto had wished me well and offered me temporary employment while I waited to enter seminary. My buddies from school and the neighborhood, too, offered their support, though they were initially taken aback. They took me out for beers as a sendoff. Only Doug reacted badly – he was a so-called Christian with fundamentalist views and an opinion that all Catholics were damned. He told me he would never talk to me again. Until that moment, I never knew his religion and he never knew mine. But suddenly, for him, our friendship had shifted. I would have to live without his approval in order to become a priest, assuming that I could become a priest.

Though I knew leaving the Army that I wanted to pursue the priesthood, I had no idea where to start. I took my questions to Father Surges, an assistant at my home parish. He remembered me from my days in the Catholic Youth Organization. I called the rectory.

"Father Surges? This is Richard Keil. I used to come to CYO," I said. "Father Surges, may I come to see you? I'm out of the Army, and I've been thinking for a long time that I would like to try to become a priest. Would you talk to me?"

"Sure, I'd be happy to see you," Father replied.

Shortly thereafter, I was ringing the doorbell of the parish rectory. The housekeeper answered the door. Everything was so quiet, beautiful and proper. I told her I was to see Father Surges. My nervousness grew.

Father was tall, had dark, curly hair and a ready smile. He was encouraging to all he met. His sermons and talks were challenging and always upbeat.

"Father Surges, I would like to try to become a priest," I said. "I realize that it is long and difficult. Do you know where I should start?"

After talking for some time, Father Surges said, "Richard, why don't you go to a place like Loras College in Dubuque or St. Thomas in Minnesota? They have seminaries and are accredited colleges. Then, if you decided not to pursue the priesthood, you could still continue your degree work in some field of study you like better."

I was overjoyed.

Father Surges excused himself and returned with addresses of the colleges. I thanked him and was on my way home. Father had been so positive and encouraging that I had no idea the life of an assistant pastor in a parish could be so miserable and regimented.

At home, I immediately wrote to the colleges, asking for admission to their seminary. Loras College sent a reply and application papers in a week or two. I also had to provide a letter of recommendation from my parish priest. I filled out the paperwork, mailed it back and was ecstatic when I received an acceptance letter.

Loras College was founded in 1839 by the Most Rev. Mathias Loras, first bishop of Dubuque – Iowa's oldest city. The school was started to educate men for the priesthood but also to offer courses to town's residents. That dual mission allowed me to hedge my bets.

So there I was, with my mother and father, headed to college in the new Ford I had bought for them with the money I had saved working at the tire store and from my Army paychecks.

When we got to Dubuque, a town with many hills on the high bluffs of the Mississippi River, we stopped and asked directions to the college, then directions to North Hall, where the seminary students lived. It was September. The leaves were brilliant and beginning to fall. I was scared. So many of the men were in black suits that the sight gave me pause. My suits were blue and brown, not black. Did I need a black suit? Would they kick me out?

It was autumn and thoughts of football, girls and Halloween came to my mind, along with a vague sense that I would have to say goodbye to all of it.

I found out where my room was and got the luggage from the car. My dad could go up to my room, but my mother had to stay downstairs. Women were not allowed out of the reception area. It was all so beautiful with red Asian rugs and walnut paneling. The building was quite new and even had marble window sills. The student rooms were immaculate, freshly painted. There was a sink in one corner, closet space, desks for two students and bunk beds. The toilets and showers were down the hall. They were finished in fine ceramic tile and marble. It was a nicer place than I was used to. I had never lived in such fine surroundings. I wondered if I was the only one for whom this was all new.

I hugged and kissed my parents goodbye. They had tears in their eyes. While they did not fully understand the Church and what was involved in becoming a priest, they did understand this: If I made it, I would be truly gone. As for me, I didn't know how much the step I was taking would pull me away from my family.

I watched my parents drive off, then sat around downstairs and watched the students coming and going. A group came in from the Dominican Novitiate on campus. I did not know anything about the Dominicans, nor did I know what a Novitiate was. They were showing me their habits of white and black cloth with long rosaries around their waists. Habits are the long outer garment that people in religious orders wear. Rosaries were the special beads that Catholics often use to keep count of prayers. I did not know much about rosaries or habits, but these guys seemed so interested in the garments' textures and colors.

It made me feel uneasy. Maybe I was in the wrong place. They seemed so girlish. I hadn't yet learned the word effeminate. I did not care about colors of robes or rosaries. I wanted to be a priest to help people, I told myself; I didn't care about the fashion. I imagined myself as a parish priest, maybe in Wisconsin.

Before long, my roommate, Harry Isbell from Dyersville, Iowa, showed up. Dyersville was a Catholic town with no public school. It produced more than its share of priests and nuns. Harry and I became friends, even though he was right out of high school. He was a smart, friendly guy, and he knew all the Catholic lingo and customs. We even chose one another for roommates the next year. He knew Latin, some Greek and all of the Catholic prayers, hymns and how to say the rosary. I knew the Our Father and Hail Mary.

But I watched, listened and learned about this new world. I learned about spiritual directors, rectors, vespers, the Mass, morning and evening prayers, meditation, the Holy Eucharist and the rosary. I studied the other seminarians and the priests. I thought of going out for the football team but concluded I needed the time for my studies. My courses mixed me with pre-med and pre-engineering students.

Monsignor Gannon, a renowned psychologist, taught one of my classes. He came in with his impressive black robes with the red trim showing that he was not just an ordinary priest but a monsignor with the formal title of Right Reverend or Very Reverend Monsignor. I was to learn that there was a big difference between Right Reverend, Very Reverend and Most Reverend. And, while I had enormous respect for the hierarchy and titles, I did not hanker to be more than a simple priest.

Father Donoghue taught freshman English. His brown hair was combed straight back and his lack of good dental care showed in his smile. His lectures were often brilliant, whether the talk was on English literature or how a clipper ship is rigged.

It was evident from his demeanor that he drank a lot. The students talked about it – we could hear his slurred speech and see his shaky stance. I would find out that his problem was not uncommon in the priesthood: There were more intelligent, good priests afflicted with alcoholism and other addictions than you could ever imagine.

My classes were English, History, Chemistry, Psychology, Religion, as well as Latin. I loved the studies, but I felt so lonely on Saturday afternoons, when football games were being played in the nearby stadium. I could hear the cheering and, from a distance, see the young guys and gals strolling on the campus. On Saturday nights, music from the dances drifted over to our seminary hall, making me wish I could hang out with a girl. No, I said to myself, you have to study and forget about girls to be a priest. Sometimes, I would cry to myself as I prayed on my knees. I told myself that, if I truly wanted to be a priest, I would pay whatever price I had to pay.

Once, as I walked to the cafeteria, I noticed a guy coming toward the seminary building. As we passed, I got a good look at this tall, black-haired, strong-looking man with a short crew cut. "Where are you from?" I asked. "Don't I know you from somewhere?"

A few minutes and a few questions later, we remembered we were in infantry basic training at Fort Ord. We laughed and were overjoyed to see that we both had decided to study for the priesthood and had chosen the same seminary. Bob began to tell me a bit of his story.

"Richard, when I was in service, I converted to Catholicism. I said the rosary every day. I read the Office of the Blessed Virgin Mary every day."

"What was your job in the service?" I asked.

"I repaired flame throwers," he replied. "It was pretty dangerous because the fuel that's used is so inflammable."

I agreed, having had a little training on how to use them.

Bob continued, "I'm an only son and my dad died early in my life. My mother is alone, and I support her. I send my GI money to my mother, and I have a scholarship to school for playing basketball and baseball."

He had a full load of classes like the rest of us and seminary training like us. He practiced three or four hours a day for varsity sports and traveled to the other colleges for games.

"Bob, I don't know how you do all of this. I am lucky just to get my studies," I said.

We continued talking. I agreed to help him with chemistry, a subject that came easy to me. We remain friends to this day.

I received a call one day from a Caleb Case. He was a Loras student but not in the seminary. He said, "Richard, I'm from Racine, and I see in the college directory that you are from Racine. Do you have a ride home for Christmas?"

"No, Caleb," I replied. "I thought I'd take the train."

"I've got a car and would be glad to give you a ride when we finish classes," he said.

I thought that it was a great offer, both for saving money and for companionship going back home, even though we didn't know each other. At Thanksgiving, I had taken the train from Dubuque to Chicago and from Chicago to Racine. It was a nice train, but so many other college students were on the train, boys and girls mixing and having fun. I felt jealous and lonely.

A couple of days later, Caleb drove up to the seminary in his new red Ford, which matched his hair. We were about the same height, but he was thinner. Caleb took my suitcase and put it in the trunk of his car. As we began our ride, we talked. I learned he was the grandson of J.I. Case, the maker of tractors distributed throughout the world. He never bragged and wasn't arrogant in talking about his family. It was just reality. We had an enjoyable ride back to Racine, and he dropped me off at my humble home.

As we said goodbye, Caleb called out, "Richard, I'm having a party after Christmas. Would you like to come?"

I was surprised. I had never socialized with people like the Cases. "Sure," I said. "I would be happy to come."

He replied, "OK, I'll call you and give you directions. It would be great if you make it."

The night of the party arrived, and I drove to the Case estate overlooking Lake Michigan. As I walked up the long driveway, I could hear waves breaking on the shore and see the Christmas decorations. Caleb greeted me at the thick wooden door of the stone home. Inside, I could hear the other guests laughing and talking. George Shearing's piano jazz was playing.

I met the other guests, but ended up conversing with a lovely college girl for much of the party. We talked about everything under the sun. Finally, we ended the evening with a kiss.

I felt guilty, but also good. The kiss had happened before I could even think about it; we seemed so close by the end of the evening, it all felt natural. I knew that, in the future, I would need to be much more careful.

CHAPTER 5

I WAS NERVOUS. A VERY well-regarded priest, Father Waldrin, was visiting Loras to lead a retreat. While I didn't quite know everything involved with a retreat, I felt that somehow it would lead to me confessing to kissing the girl at the Christmas party and the impure thoughts that followed.

This holy man would surely see that I wasn't fit to be a priest, I thought. Still, there was no avoiding it. I was expected to attend the retreat, just as everyone else was.

I don't remember the retreat's theme. Father Waldrin gave his talks to the group, then met individually with the seminarians. One after another came out of his session, shaking his head and saying Father Waldrin had advised him to strongly consider leaving the seminary. I thought I, too, would be asked to rethink my goal.

After knocking on the door and hearing his gentle, "Come in," I entered the office, furnished with an Asiatic rug, a mahogany desk and a couple of upholstered sitting chairs. A crucifix hung on the wall as it did in every room in the seminary.

"Thank you for seeing me, Father Waldrin. I wish to go to confession and to ask your advice and counsel about being a seminarian," I stammered.

I went on. "Bless me, Father, for I have sinned. My last confession was a few weeks ago and these are my sins since then." I started reciting my list of sins and continued straight into the part about kissing the girl at the party. Father listened to me and gave no reaction. Finally I asked him, "Should I leave the seminary?"

"No, Richard," he replied. "I think that you will be a fine priest. Continue to pray, study and do your best."

I was relieved and happy to receive his affirmation. I had been honest with him, and it turned out that my weakness at the party was not enough to end my journey to the priesthood. Besides, it turned out, the seminary would be supplying us with advisers to help us overcome spiritual challenges.

Each of us seminarians was assigned a priest to act as a personal spiritual director. They picked for me Father William Most, a well-known scholar who wrote Latin textbooks. His books would include nursery rhymes like "Mary Had a Little Lamb." He had a whole new way of teaching Latin. Father Most also wrote about the role of Jesus' mother. He was what is called a Mariologist. In 1954, a book he authored was named by Pope Pius XII as the best book about Mary.

Father Most was short and was called "Ducky Most" by the students. He was scholarly, introverted and seemingly not comfortable talking about personal issues. But he was ever kind and gentlemanly. When I went to see him, he would look up from his mountain of books, push up his green plastic visor and make small talk with a nervous laugh. I felt he wanted be a good adviser, but was more at home with his books and writing.

In time, I decided to ask Father Vogl, the spiritual director of the seminary, to be my personal spiritual director. He was friendly, very strict with himself and gave the impression that he expected much of other priests and seminarians. His sitting room was always immaculate, with every paper and book in its place. He was balding and wore rimless glasses. His black suits were always well pressed. I shared with him my experiences with the girl at the party and other struggles in my life and asked him, too, if I should leave the seminary.

"Richard, not only do I think that you should stay, but that you will be an excellent priest," Father Vogl said. "If you would like, maybe you could go somewhere during the summer that would be more conducive to living a life of a seminarian. Maybe you could help at your local parish during the short vacations."

I considered Father Vogl's advice and began to think of ways to embrace my new life as a seminarian and future life as a priest.

Easter marked our next vacation home. Back in Racine, I went over to the rectory to see Father Surges, who had first steered me to Loras College. "Father Surges, I would like to spend my time at home more productively," I told him. "I was wondering if I could help around the parish. I can do a lot of things, including cleaning or painting."

Father Surges went back to the pastor's office. In a few minutes, the pastor, Monsignor Richard Schaefer, came out to the parlor. We did not know one another. I had seen him and heard his sermons many times. He was a large man, polished and in charge.

"Father Surges told me that you are a seminarian and want to help in the parish during vacation time," he began. "How much do you want to be paid?"

"Monsignor, I don't want to be paid," I said. "I have the GI Bill that helps me with expenses. I just want to occupy my time with positive things."

Monsignor smiled. "I understand. We need to have our church cleaned, waxed and polished for Easter. We have a large church. Will it be too much for you?"

Knowing the size of the church, I said, "No. Why don't I begin and we can see how it goes. If you or someone else can give me some directions, equipment and materials, I will get started today."

Monsignor beamed. "You can start today? That would be an immense help. The floor is an expensive terrazzo marble, and it would look beautiful if it was cleaned and polished."

When I finished the floor, I was proud to see the pink, green, yellow and other colors that were hidden under the dirt. The wax made the surface shine and sparkle. The Monsignor was ecstatic. I asked him if he had more work to do.

"Do you really mean that?" he asked.

"Yes," I replied. I was having fun, helping others and staying out of trouble.

"Some school classrooms need painting," the pastor said. "Do you know how to paint?"

I replied I'd be happy to try my best in the time I had left during my Easter break.

In an hour, some paint, brushes, rollers, ladders and drop clothes appeared, and I began. Painting classrooms seemed more challenging than cleaning and polishing floors. Sisters, priests, parents and students would be taking a close look at classrooms.

Early the next morning, I returned to the school and there was a Dominican sister with her white and black religious habit. "Good morning. I am Sister Coronata. What's your name?"

I introduced myself.

"Monsignor Schaefer told me that a young seminarian had offered to paint some classrooms," she said. "We are so happy and grateful to you."

"I'm happy to be here to help," I said. "But you may want to wait on being grateful. I may not be so welcomed after you see my work. What grade do you teach?"

Sister replied, "I teach the eighth grade and am also the principal."

"You have a difficult job," I said. "Who is the Sister Superior?"

"I am the Superior. The other sisters would like to meet you and thank you. Would you have a minute now?"

I was surprised to be so welcomed. "Thank you, sister. I would love to meet them."

In a few minutes, several sisters came into the room. Sister Coronata began to introduce them.

"This is Sister Valeria", she said, pointing to an elderly, stocky woman with twinkling eyes behind rimless glasses. We shook hands and laughed about something.

I turned to the others and couldn't help thinking how young they seemed. Sister Kevin was statuesque and quiet. Sister Mary Ellen was uninhibited and animated, readily expressing her mind. Sister Rebecca was angelic looking and chose her words carefully. I would go on to develop deeply meaningful friendships with these sisters through the years.

After greeting each of them, I got back to my painting job and finished one classroom after another. Once in a while, a plate of cookies and orange juice would be delivered by a sister. I marveled at the gracefulness and cheer of these young women living a life of poverty, chastity and obedience. Each of them was attractive, talented and highly motivated. These were powerful women, I told myself, "If these young ladies can be so focused for God, I surely can sacrifice myself and give myself fully to God."

Easter vacation ended, and I felt good going back to school. I had spent my time being productive.

At Loras, I knocked at Father Vogl's door. "Father, may I see you?"

"Yes, Richard, I have been looking forward to seeing you. You spoke to me about having a place to go during summer vacation that would be conducive for your life as a seminarian. I wrote to a former classmate who is part of a religious order in the South. He wrote back to me saying that they may have some opening in Alabama, where they have a seminary, church and farm. Here is his name and address."

"Thanks so much, Father Vogl. I'll write him tonight," I said.

I looked at the information: Father Norbert Sharon, M.S.Ss.T. These initials seemed formidable. The address was Holy Trinity, Alabama.

I told Father Norbert in my letter that I wanted to spend the summer constructively, perhaps teaching the Bible to the kids in the area. The reply from Father Norbert was welcoming, but he stated the only work they could provide would be on the farm, doing manual labor around the seminary. There would be no pay. I needed to get to Alabama on my own. Meals and a place to sleep would be provided.

I was not looking for money. I had saved enough from my Army days and a job I had at the Loras College laundry. I decided to go to Alabama.

School ended with my grades improving each quarter. I packed for my trip and pulled out a map. In tiny lettering, I saw the words Holy Trinity. I would be gone for roughly three months. In the Army, I had heard about the cockroaches, the poverty in the South. Somewhere, I had learned of Jim Crow laws.

I got my tickets for the Northwestern 400 train to Chicago, then walked several blocks with my suitcase to the Illinois Central Station. My mother had put some sandwiches in my bag, and I bought some candy bars for the trip. I found my seat in the coach section and settled in for the long overnight trip into the Deep South.

CHAPTER 6

As THE TRAIN SNAKED ITS way through Chicago and gained speed outside the city limits, I noticed a number of black people among the passengers. The train chugged through the Illinois plains, past farmland with corn sprouting out of rich black soil, and the announcer rattled off the names of the cities and towns where stops were scheduled.

Dozing in and out, I heard the railroad crossing bells, the train's horn and the clickity clack of the train on the track. People got up to go to the restrooms or dining car. I took a stroll or two, but mostly snoozed, read and thought.

The farther south we went, the fewer passengers there were in my car. As passengers left, not as many new passengers were getting on. Empty seats were all around me when we arrived in Atlanta, where I switched trains. Then I saw signs on some of the cars – "Colored Only." I was taken aback by this introduction to Jim Crow, even though, logically, I should have known it was coming.

Pulling into Columbus, Georgia, the car I was riding in was way down the track. I had to walk on crushed gravel for several hundred feet before arriving at the concrete platform. It was stunningly hot. I had never felt heat like this. I was to meet Father Norbert in the station. I looked for a Roman collar, but saw no one who resembled a priest. People came and went from the inbound trains, then I was almost alone in the station.

There were signs – "White," "Colored" – and clear divisions of labor. Black people were doing the lifting and hard work. White people sold the tickets. The atmosphere seemed a bit tense, with everyone knowing his or her place and watching to make sure others obeyed the rules.

Father Norbert did not show up, so I asked a cab driver if he knew of a place called Holy Trinity.

"No, suh, I never did hear of that," he said.

Two women in black dresses walked into the station and looked around. They did not look like Catholic sisters, but I took a chance and asked if they had heard of Holy Trinity. They smiled. "Are you Richard Keil? Father Norbert couldn't make it, and he asked if we would meet you."

Happy to see them, I responded, "Yes, I'm Richard. I am glad to meet you."

"I'm Sister Rita," the taller sister said. "And this is Sister Alphonsus." Both were elderly and gray. They wore black dresses, black felt hats and black stockings and shoes. No long habits like other sisters.

We gathered the luggage and headed for the car. When we began to move, they began to pray. I almost panicked. It seemed too holy-roller. The sisters smiled and explained that, in the Trinitarian Congregation, there was a rule that required the members to pray whenever a trip began, long or short.

"We have to stop to get groceries," one of them said. "Do you want to go with us?"

"Yes, I'd be happy to," I responded, thinking I could carry their groceries. I quickly got out of the car, opened the sister's door and stepped on her insole.

"Oh, Sister, I'm so sorry," I said.

Sister quickly said, "No, Brother, It's OK. I'm fine." It wasn't a good way to start off in this strange land.

After getting groceries at Big Apple, one sister asked me, "Would you like to get an ice cream cone?"

Now they were talking about something I could handle. We all got ice cream, and life began to look better.

We traveled on Front Avenue past the corporate offices of W.C. Bradley. Bradley had invested in Coca Cola, chaired its board and hired the famous Robert Woodruff to head the company. There was Kinfolks Corner, where black people would congregate for refreshments or to share a ride back into rural Alabama. It was a study of profound contrasts, rich and poor, privileged and outcast. A bridge took us from Columbus to Phenix City, Alabama. We drove down Seale Road and passed Sumbry's Funeral Home.

One sister quietly whispered to me, "That's where the NAACP meets, but no one is supposed to know. It's for colored people."

Driving down Seale Road, I saw small homes, old cars with no tires in the yards, shabby clothes fluttering on clotheslines, and people walking down the sides of the road. The small stores advertised Bull Durham, Lucky Strikes, Moon Pies, Coke and RC Cola. I knew of Lucky Strikes and Coke and maybe even RC, but Bull Durham and Moon Pies were foreign to me.

We drove until we came to a bridge. Sister Rita said, "Holy Trinity begins here with all of these pine trees on both sides of the road. In some minutes, we will come to a clearing. That is Red Level, which is part of the farm. I used to be in charge of the farm. I would ride my horse and shoot stray dogs that were after our livestock and keep out stray cows and pigs."

I could not have imagined how large it was. We came to a well-manicured lawn with a long driveway lined with cedar trees. At the end was a circle with a statue of St. Joseph holding the Christ Child. In back of the driveway was a chapel, all framed, with white shingles. We went inside, and the sisters knelt down to pray. They informed me that they always visited the chapel before and after leaving Holy Trinity. I prayed myself, asking for help and guidance.

In a few minutes, a brother appeared. "Hi, I'm Brother Eugene. Father Norbert meant to pick you up, but all of the priests were called out to say Mass," he explained. "There are not many priests in the South, and the priests here at the seminary help out in many places like Albany, Fort Benning, Montgomery, Eufaula and Union Springs.

"May I help you with your luggage? We can get you settled and maybe get you something to eat. You must be tired and hungry after all of this travel."

Brother Eugene's manners were gracious, his diction perfect.

Sister Rita said, "Richard, it was good to meet you, and I hope you enjoy your summer at Holy Trinity."

They drove off to their convent down the road.

"Richard, you will be staying by yourself in the college dorm, which is really an old army barracks. There are many rooms on the ground floor. You can just pick a room. There is a common bathroom."

I looked around at my new home. It was large and made of wood. The second floor had classrooms and a colloquy room where students could relax. It was clean, old and sparsely furnished. There was another barracks on the campus and other large, one-story buildings. One building served as a dormitory for the high school students, one for priests and brothers, and there was the refectory, where everyone ate. Another building was the infirmary, and there was an oratory with many altars. Holy Trinity was a little city with its own laundry, water works and maintenance shops. The old plantation seemed peaceful and sacred.

Father Thomas Augustine Judge bought the 1,445 acres for $12,000 after the turn of the century. Until then, the priests, brothers and sisters all lived on another plantation. Everyone stayed in the old milk barn, with sheets hung on the cow stanchions to separate men from women.

I put sheets on the old army bed and my clothes in the worn dresser. Brother Eugene then came back and called down the hall, "Are you ready for something to eat? I'll take you to the refectory."

At the time, I did not know what a refectory, oratory (a place to pray), colloquy room (a place to talk and relax) and dozens of other terms meant. We walked into a large empty room with tables set for many to eat. Brother and I sat down and a black woman came out and served us.

She smiled. "Hi, Brother," she said as we started to eat. "How's you?"

"I am fine, Corine. How are you?" Brother Eugene replied. "This is Richard Keil. He will be with us for much of the summer."

Corine smiled and said, "Hello, Brother Richard. How's you?"

"Thank you, madam, I am fine. Thank you for the wonderful food." I wasn't just being polite – the chicken, potatoes, corn bread, vegetables, ice tea and cherry pie were out of this world.

Corine was dark, so black she was almost a shade of blue. Later, some priests and brothers told me that black people as dark as Corine were especially backward, having come from Africa at a different time and from a different place than other black people in the South. I felt uncomfortable about their words, but knew nothing about the truth. Of course, many of the black people were lighter shades – cream, brown or yeller, as they were called. I did know enough to know the light shades came from white folk. I learned later that these priests and brothers were just plain wrong in their views.

That evening, some of the priests began to return to Holy Trinity from their Sunday assignments. I met Father Norbert. He was a short, handsome priest with an eager smile.

"Hi, Richard. It's so great to have you. Brother Eugene told me you are settled in the college dorm. It's luxury at its finest!" he laughed. "I hope this heat is not too much for you – or seeing this seminary in the Old South. It's sure not that nice Loras College in Dubuque.

"I went to Loras College," he continued. "My daddy owned a lumber company there, and I wanted to serve the poor so I came south to join the Trinitarians. I'm so glad you're here. We don't have money. You will be of immense help."

Father Norbert could have been the PR person for Coca Cola, it seemed. He knew how to smile, laugh, talk, think, work and get things done. He was complimenting me, and I had done nothing yet.

Lessons Along the Way

"How would you like me to help and when do we get started?" I asked.

He recited the schedule. "We get up at 5:30 and have prayers, meditation and Mass. Then we have more prayers, and we go to eat. We can meet here about 8:15 a.m. Is that OK?"

That was a lot to get done by 8:15, but I had signed up for this. "Fine, I will see you tomorrow."

"Richard, I am Father Killian," came a soft, serious voice.

Father Norbert interceded, "This is Father Killian, the Custodian of Holy Trinity. He is the Superior over all of the priests and brothers."

I was nervous as I extended my hand. "It's good to meet you, Father Killian."

Father Killian was of medium height, about 45, 50 years old, gray hair, with light plastic rimmed glasses. I would come to have much admiration for this extremely conservative and prayerful priest. Many criticized him as being too ascetic, but I didn't agree. He was the Superior of a large religious house, and religious life was very restrictive.

There was a good bit of drinking among the priests and brothers. Father Killian did not like it and used to mark the whiskey bottles. But that never worked. Then he personally locked the liquor in his room and brought it out before dinner.

At first, I thought these were extreme measures. But later – after I was ordained and began to interact with many different priests – I came to appreciate his attempt to address the problem. It was an ineffectual way to go about interacting with alcoholics, but he had few choices as he tried to change the culture of his religious order.

CHAPTER 7

IT WAS 8 A.M., AND the sun was already high in the sky. I had on old jeans, a T-shirt and sneakers. I was ready to sweat. Today, I was to meet the local laborers who worked for us. Father Norbert greeted me. He was upbeat and neatly dressed.

"How did you sleep last night? Did you get enough to eat for breakfast?" he asked.

I assured him that I had and did.

"Richard, I am so glad you're here. We have so much to do and so little money and assistance to get it done. We want to serve people who need us, and we have so little help."

Two black laborers had arrived.

"We are building a barn, and these two nice fellows are showing us how. Right, Esau?" Father Norbert said.

They quickly replied yes.

Father introduced me to Esau Hartman Sr. and Esau Hartman Jr. When I extended my hand to Esau Hartman Sr., he took off his hat, looked down and said, "Yes, suh, Brother. Yes, suh." He hesitantly offered his hand. It was as if he thought something was wrong with us touching. He had gray hair and gray whiskers. His skin was as black as Corine's. He was bent over from years of hard manual work.

"Yes, suh, Brother" was repeated several times as I told him I was happy to meet him. I felt there was something deep about him and wondered about the hard times I was sure he had seen. This man is beautiful, I thought. He can teach me so much. He reads my sincerity, too, I thought at the time, I can tell. Who knows what Esau was really thinking.

In time, after working side by side for many days, he told me the story of how his back came to be so bent and why he moved so slowly. He would talk of carrying sacks of feed off the riverboats while being watched and teased by a guard with a shotgun, sitting high on a perch.

"Get yo' ass moving, boy. I say, get yo' ass moving!" the guard would yell at him. The guard was hired to make sure people like Esau never slacked off, not even for a moment.

I realized I was getting conflicting messages. Some white people had told me blacks were lazy, immoral and dirty. Here was an old gentleman, in a nice clean shirt and overalls. He was there to work for $3 a day. It was the beginning of my education on the black community. I was learning and not from books by white authors, Northern or Southern. This teacher was authentic. I was blessed to have this precious man instructing me in his patient way.

Many years later, I read a book written by the grandson of the owner of the riverboats and plantations on which Esau worked for starvation wages, a back-breaking job with thousands of other poor people. The grandson is fabulously wealthy, and the empire is worth billions. This sincere but unknowing grandson talked with pride about the great works and deeds of his grandfather. His language was almost religious-sounding in its praise. How little he seemed to understand that his grandfather got rich off the backs of the poor.

As I began to work on the barn, Esau's son showed me how to shovel the right mix for concrete. Was it three shovels of stone, two of sand, one of concrete then add water?

Mixing cement in 95 to 100 degree temperatures, pouring it into wheelbarrows, carting it to where we were laying sidewalks, I kept in shape. Esau Sr. would smooth the cement with his trowel.

I said to Esau Sr. something to the effect, "This is like my work in the Army." He said to me, "Hush yo' mouth, Brother." I was taken aback. "Hush your mouth" was on the harsh side, and I could tell that Esau was a very kind man. I was puzzled. Then I got it. He was surprised to know that I had been in the Army. I was learning a lesson a minute.

Day in and day out, we worked until we were at the point of putting on the barn's roof. Because I was young and agile, I worked at pounding nails into the higher parts of the barn, not worried about a thing. I was working with Esau Jr., with him showing me many carpentry skills. I balanced on a skimpy 2-by-8 and shimmied down low enough to get another board from Esau Sr.

"Brother, suh," he said one day, "be careful when I give you the board and don't drop it before I can run out of the way."

I responded, "Mr. Hartman, I will be very careful."

He stopped and said, "I am not a mister," insisting that he was just an old nigger. I have thought and thought about this moment, and 60 or so years later, it still burns in my heart. The memory of that moment later helped to inspire me to begin the Tubman Museum in Macon to help change the low self-image of some African-American children and to portray the African-American community in a dignified way.

When I took the board from Esau Sr., I waited as he had asked before carrying it up the roof. I thought he would quickly get out of the way. He just slowly moved his body. From that vantage point, I could clearly see what years of endless toil, and being 73, did to a body. At first, I laughed to myself, "God, this guy moves really slowly. I mean really slowly." Then I reflected on the realities of the situation and felt ashamed.

Esau Sr. had many grandchildren, and I asked him if they liked to swim. He said, "No, suh, Brother. There is no place for kids to swim in this area."

I inquired around, asking the priests and brothers, knowing that there was a lake and a pool on the Trinitarian property. The swimming pool at Holy Trinity was high on a hill near the big water reservoir. A well supplied water for all of Holy Trinity. I learned that the pool was for the priests and brothers, and on rare occasions, the sisters would request privacy and go up there and swim. Sometimes, white friends of some of the priests and brothers would come to swim. The black people of the area were not allowed in the pool. The priests and brothers said they had multiple reasons. Their spoken reason was that insurance did not cover outside people. However, outside whites came and went. At lunch or dinner, the unofficial reason came out. In those conversations, some of the priests would say that black people were dirty, carried infections and were generally not trustworthy.

The younger black teenagers working on the barn and in the fields began to push a bit more. "Brother," they asked me, "since we can't swim in the pool, would you let us swim in the lake?"

The lake on the property was part of the farm and was located in some pasture.

I told Johnny Johnson and Mose Thornton, the two teens asking me, "That's a great idea, but I have no power here. I'm not in the religious order."

Thinking about their request, I later went to Father Killian, the religious superior. He had close to absolute power in the day-to-day running of Holy Trinity. He was a former A&P store manager, a very prayerful and meditative man. He said, "Richard, I don't know if it's a good thing. Something could happen and someone could drown. Maybe too many people would come from all over to swim in the lake and hurt our property. I will pray over it."

I said to Father, "I will go swimming with the teens and children after work each night and then go to night prayers."

"I'll pray about it," Father Killian repeated.

The next morning after prayers, Mass, breakfast and more prayers, Father Killian approached me and said, "Richard, I have prayed over your request. It will be OK to swim with the kids in the lake, if you take them there in the truck, lifeguard and watch over them. Then take them home and come to night prayers."

I was thrilled.

I could hardly wait to finish the workday. At 4:30 p.m., I ran up from the barn, got on my swimming suit, grabbed a towel and jumped into the old GMC truck. It was a two-ton truck with wooden sides and a large bed. We could put a lot of kids back there. I drove down to Norbertville and collected dozens of kids who had gotten the word out that Brother Keil was going swimming with them. We bumped along the dirt road, dodging trees and limbs, the kids laughing and singing and talking. The swimming suits were old and, in some cases, just shorts or cut-off trousers. The girls were in suits that seemed to be one size fits all.

When we got to Lonesome Duck Lake, we were all aware of the water moccasins. I warned everyone to keep a watch out.

"Hey, Brother, teach me to swim," said one of the younger kids while the older ones were splashing in the water. Only a few knew how to swim. There had been no opportunity to learn. Here I was with this mass of kids, playing among water moccasins, with very few swimmers and me as the only lifeguard and swim teacher.

I noticed Mose and Johnny swimming very well. "Hey, you guys are great," I yelled. They smiled and came over to me.

"Can you help these bigger boys and girls learn to swim while I watch the little ones?" I asked.

"Sure, Brother, we can do that if they aren't too dumb," came the teasing reply.

We all splashed and swam, laughed and shouted in the torrid late afternoon heat. As we climbed back into the truck and bounced down the dirt road, again watching for the low limbs, loving parents waved to us. They wore looks of gratitude and goodness. It was the first of many happy days for me, living and learning from the local community.

Esau Sr. and I talked for hours as we worked. I learned much from him. One day, he found a raccoon in a metal garbage can. The mammal had climbed in to get the garbage and couldn't get out. Esau told me it would make a fine meal for his family.

After work, he and his son put a stout round wire on the end of a hoe handle. Then the elderly man told his son to hold the handle and to be ready to put the wire about the raccoon's neck when he pulled it out of the garbage can. The raccoon was raging inside the can, and I didn't know how he would safely pick up the raccoon without being bitten or losing a finger or two.

He just stood by the pail and began talking to the raccoon and humming softly. Then, ever so slowly, he let his arm drop into the garbage can with the raccoon scurrying about and gnashing its teeth. This went on for what I thought was the longest time, with the talking, humming, snarling and gnashing of teeth, with Esau continuing to lower his arm, all as cool as can be. The raccoon was finally silent, and Esau Sr. quickly grabbed it by the neck. The raccoon hissed, fighting mad. Esau told his son to put the wire hook around the raccoon's neck, and they twisted the wire until it was snug. Then Esau Jr. grabbed the hoe handle, and they proceeded to walk down the road with the fighting raccoon walking behind. The whole process was impressive to me, and I was awestruck by the skills and the bravery of Esau Sr.

Once, while we were talking, I asked him how he got to be such a good person. He said, "Oh, Brother, I ain't good, and I used to be a bad one, until my wife died."

"How is that so? What happened?"

Esau went on to tell me that he and his wife had seven children. He drank and smoked, gambled and carried on. Then his wife died, leaving him with the children. He was completely lost and baffled as to how he would cope. This was the late '20s and '30s, during the Depression.

"Brother, I didn't know what to do, except cry and drink. I was about to give up. Then one day I said I was going into the woods to live until I got a sign from God. I wandered three days.

"It began to lightning, thunder, with the wind blowing and raining so hard, I was afraid. But I just prayed. Finally, I promised God that I would reform if he would send me a sign. I said, 'God, do you see those three tall trees over there? If you would send lightning and strike the middle tree, I will never smoke, drink, gamble or chase women again. I will go home and raise my children like you want.' Well, sure 'nough, Brother, I was watching the sky and a huge bolt of lightning came down and struck the tree, and thunder rattled everything in the woods. I fell to my knees, frightened, and thanked God and made my promise. I went home, and I never drank, smoked, gambled or chased women. I have raised my children to be good and got them schooled."

The old man's tale of redemption lasted about two hours.

I never repeated that story to the people in the religious order because they would have laughed and ridiculed it. I thought it was no different than the experiences of other people when they have religious conversions. People seemed to embrace stories more like those of Clare Booth Luce, an accomplished woman who converted to Catholicism after the death of her daughter and extensive counseling from a bishop. But it's Esau's story that has always been a source of encouragement and awe to me. Esau died years ago at age 79.

CHAPTER 8

THE SOUTH WAS AT WAR when I arrived there. In fact, the whole country was, but I was blithely unaware.

It was the summer of 1956. Two years earlier, the Supreme Court had declared racially segregated schools unconstitutional, sparking outrage among whites throughout the region. One state over to the west, a black teenager from Chicago, Emmett Till, had been brutally murdered by white men in Money, Mississippi, leaving the African-American community clamoring for justice. Just 95 miles to the east, a black woman had refused to give up her seat on a bus to a white passenger, a decision that led to her arrest and the Montgomery Bus Boycott, which had been going on for more than half a year at that point.

Here I was, a husky 5-foot-7, 22-year-old Army veteran, a product of Wisconsin public schools, a second-year Catholic seminarian, trying to spend a summer away from temptations to drink or chase women. I was in the rural South, but was caught off guard by the racial undertow.

On a blistering July day, I was walking around the farm that belonged to the Trinitarian religious order, feeling good but tired and sweaty after working outside mixing cement for a new barn floor. I was hurrying to my room in the old army barracks to change into my swimming suit and pick up the children who lived near the seminary for a swimming outing. In the old days of sharecropping, I was told, there would be about 14 black families living and working the farm. As I passed the building that housed the mission dedicated to the black people of the area, the door of the small white frame rectory opened and Father Francis called out to me.

"Hi, Doc."

"Hi, Father Francis."

"Hey, Doc, come here for a second."

This priest called everyone "Doc." Father Francis was short, pudgy and friendly. He could have been good looking with less weight. His light hair was receding. Someone told me that he had an advanced theology degree from Rome and was a professor in the seminary.

"Doc, I'm here for the summer, filling in for Father Bernadine. He's the regular pastor of this Godforsaken mission," he said in his native New Jersey accent. "The teenagers are supposed to take a trip to Panama City next Tuesday. I noticed that you like the niggers around here. If I asked Father Killian, the superior, would you chaperone them for the day? I don't want to go with them."

I was taken aback. Sure, I had heard people say nasty things about black people before. I had heard the word nigger thrown around by ignorant white people who also would spew opinions about the inferiority of blacks and their lack of moral and intellectual capacity. Yet it often caught me off guard, especially when it came from clergy. I was at Holy Trinity, the founding place of the Trinitarian religious order. I was stunned he had used the slur, not even bothering to think of some lame euphemism, but I didn't address his ignorance. I reasoned that he was afraid of black people and probably anyone else not the same as him.

"I would love to go, Father Francis, if Father Killian will give his permission," I quickly said.

I wondered how it was possible that this priest was assigned to a black mission.

"Good, Doc. I will fix it up so you can go. Just make sure you don't get into any trouble."

"Father Francis, all will be fine. Thanks a lot for asking," I replied, genuinely happy and smiling at what I considered my good fortune.

After swimming with the children at the lake and eating supper, I was on my way to night prayers at the oratory. Father Killian stopped me and said, "Father Francis asked me if you could chaperone the mission teen club on the trip to Panama City. He said that he had some important business he had to take care of. He thought that you might like to go. Would you like to go? You would be good at it."

I immediately said, "Yes, Father Killian. I would be happy to go." Naively, I wondered what important business had come up for Father Francis. I did not think much of it. I was just happy for the trust Father Killian put in me and for the opportunity to meet more of the teenagers and to spend time with them.

The Tuesday morning of the Panama City trip came, and I woke excited and happy. At 5:30 a.m., I attended morning prayers with the priests and brothers, then Mass. Father Killian gave me permission to skip the formal meditation period to fix myself an early breakfast.

I walked into the refectory, the dining place, and noticed a single place set with juice, toast, ham and coffee. I wondered why the place was set, and, at that moment, I saw the beautiful faces of Corine Adams, Leila Mae Lockhart and Leila Mae Alexander, the women who cooked, cleaned and did the laundry for the priests and brothers.

Leila Mae Lockhart was the mother of Corine Adams and Leila Mae Alexander and three other children. She was old even in 1956, and often told the story of seeing the first car coming down Highway 165. She was thin and elderly, but her beautiful black skin showed few wrinkles. Her smile reflected some shiny gold teeth. And her speech, while slow, was deliberate and authoritative. Of her three sons, two inherited this dignified speech pattern and were remarkable public speakers.

Corine Adams was married to Bill Adams and had five children. As the years passed, the two of them, along with the younger Leila Mae and their brother, Paul Anthony Lockhart, would become beloved friends and helpers.

Corine smiled saying, "Good morning, Brother Keil. We have breakfast ready for you. Father Killian told us that you were leaving early this morning with the teen club from the mission."

"That's wonderful," I said. "You shouldn't have done that. I could have gotten breakfast for myself. Thanks so much."

The elder Leila Mae said, "We're so happy you're going with our children and teen club to Panama City. Brother Keil, we are proud of you!"

I could feel the love of these women because I had agreed to take the children of the community on this trip. I cry as I write this, because I am so grateful to them for helping me be accepted by the black community of rural Alabama.

"Thanks so much for making me breakfast," I said when I finished my meal. "It was perfect."

They smiled and expressed their joy at being able to help me. I went back to my room in the barracks, put on my swim trunks under my jeans and grabbed my hat and sunglasses. I knelt down before Father Killian to get his blessing before I left, as is the practice of the Trinitarian Order. He blessed me, moving his right arm in the form of a cross and saying, "May God the Father, Son and Holy Spirit bless you now and forever and keep you safe, Richard."

"Thank you, Father Killian, for letting me go with the teen club," I said.

"Here is $10, Richard, in case you need money."

I thought it was nice of him to offer me money for something I wanted to do. I said, "Oh no, Father Killian, I have money."

"Richard, take the money."

"Yes, Father. Thank you very much, Father."

Out the door I went and walked toward the St. Peter Claver Mission to meet the teens for our trip. The sun was coming up fast. It was about 7 a.m. I was thinking about who might go on the trip. I really didn't know many of the teens except Mose, Johnny and a few others who went swimming with us after work.

I could see a group of people gathered around the old yellow mission bus that was spattered with red clay and marred with scratches and dents. As I approached, I noticed some people who were definitely not teenagers. I thought they must have been there to see the teens off. How wrong I was. I didn't understand the significance of a rural black community in 1956 taking a trip to Panama City. Aunts, uncles, grandmothers, grandfathers, cousins and elementary school children were also coming. There were boxes of food, picnic baskets, towels, sunglasses, hats, a tub of ice for drinks and a lot of laughing and talking.

I noticed that one teenager was going to each person, collecting money and organizing to get the show on the road. She came up to me and said, "Good morning, Brother Keil. I'm Thelma. Thank you for coming with us." I looked at her and saw a friendly and beautiful person. She continued talking with a couple of other people, giving some light-hearted instructions, then said to me, "We're so grateful. Father Francis would not let us go without a chaperone. We were afraid that we would have to cancel the trip."

I noticed that Thelma had rare social skills. She was as comfortable with me as she was with the other teenagers and grandmothers. She had the respect of her peers, male and female. I had never met a person who could lead by putting others so at ease. Yes, I was surprised to find this in Russell County, Alabama. It was one of dozens of lessons I was to learn that day.

Thelma went around and asked everyone to get on the bus. Paul Anthony Lockhart was the driver. He spoke kindly to each person, young or old as they boarded the bus. "Good morning, Mr. Williams. Good morning, Mrs. Thornton. Good morning, Mose. Good morning, Marie. Good morning, Brother Keil."

Paul was short and muscular. His front teeth had a wide gap; his face was square and handsome. He had an easy, gentle way that I was to witness many times. We were ready to start our trip to Panama Beach, children, teens, grandparents.

Paul Anthony started the bus, and Thelma asked me to say a prayer. I noticed the sincere devotion of the people onboard. The bus coughed a bit, and Paul laughed and joked about whether it would make it to Panama City. Paul knew the old bus would make it, but he also knew it would take some coaxing on the way. He did not tell me beforehand about the coaxing that likely would be needed.

As we began to roll down the highway, I went up and down the aisle meeting people, trying to keep names straight. I wanted to show my interest in each person and give him or her a chance to know me. I was a white person, and I was beginning to understand that many white people were not nice to black people. I wanted to be a brother to each person.

Most of the people on the bus knew each other. They knew the area. They knew what they could say in front of whom and what might be better left unsaid. We were rolling down Highway 165, planning to stop for last-minute supplies, when we passed Mr. C.D.'s store. I heard someone say, "There's Mr. C.D's place. Don't stop there." A few people chimed in, "Yeah, not there."

I didn't make much of it at the moment, but I began to think. Mr. C.D. had let me use his phone recently when my truck had broken down. I was carrying a load of lumber to Eufaula, and the truck decided to quit. I got out and walked to the country store. It was crowded with RC Cola and Coke signs; an old refrigerator holding food; shelves with cigarettes, salve and a lot of dusty items that hadn't sold in years. A man with a gray crew cut stood among it all. He was sinewy and thin and reserved in his greeting. There were a couple of black people on the outside of the store in the back, and he barked several orders at them. I assumed they worked for him.

"I'm from Holy Trinity up the road, and my truck broke down. I'm Richard," I said. "May I use the phone to call Father Norbert?"

Hearing the name Father Norbert, the man's expression perked up and he smiled slightly. "Now that Father Norbert, he's quite somebody, ain't he?"

"Yes. Do you know him?" I asked.

"Yes sir, I know all them priests up there at Holy Trinity," he said. "I've been good to all of them. They don't know how to treat the niggers though. Would you have a drink of liquor? I won't tell anyone." He smiled in a teasing way, but maybe not so teasing.

"Thanks, but I have to get the lumber to Eufaula, and I need help to get the truck going," I said, politely trying to dodge the education he wanted to give on how black people should be treated. "But may I use the phone?"

"I ain't got nary a phone here, but go up to the house and my wife will let you use the phone to call. By the way, I'm C.D., and I am too glad to help you."

"Thank you, Mr. C.D.," I said, as I turned to go out the door. I walked up to the well-kept grounds and gardens to the house and knocked on the door. A black woman answered. She had a neat appearance and wore a white dress, like a nurse.

"May I help you, sir?"

"Hi, thank you. I'm Richard from Holy Trinity, and Mr. C.D. said I could use the phone to call Holy Trinity. My truck broke down."

The woman let me in and replied, "Please wait, and I will get Mrs. C.D."

I waited a few minutes and soon a well-dressed, distinguished looking woman, came into the room. "Good morning," she said. "I am Mrs. C.D. Mae said that you needed to use the phone." As I looked around the old but well-kept home, I admired the hardwood floors and antique furniture. I knew nothing of antiques and the other lovely things I was seeing.

"I'm Richard Keil from Holy Trinity. I need to call Father Norbert to help me get the truck running."

She said, "Oh, Father Norbert! He is such a wonderful man. We all love the priests, brothers and sisters at Holy Trinity. They don't understand many of us more genteel people in the South, but they are good neighbors. They just don't deal with the colored right. Here, come in the kitchen and you may use the phone."

Mrs. C.D. led me to the kitchen, and I called Father Norbert. He said that he would send Brother McNair to help me. I thanked Father and hung up. Mrs. C.D. then said, "Come into the front room, and we will wait for Brother to come."

We sat in the parlor, and I could see pictures of her grown daughters and one son. They were beautiful like their mother. Everything was polished and dusted. A couple of times, Mrs. C.D called to the black maid, Mae, giving her directions, with the maid saying, "Yes ma'am," "no ma'am." It was clear why the house was so clean and immaculate. Mae kept it that way. It was also clear that Mrs. C.D. ruled with an iron fist, with no chance of the maid even slightly disagreeing with her. This was apparently what she and Mr. C.D. meant when they talked about the right way to treat black people.

Mrs. C.D. proceeded to tell me more about herself. "I'm from a fine family in Texas. I met Mr. C.D. after he had sown his wild oats."

I asked the meaning of "sown wild oats."

She was surprised and smiled. She said, "That's what a young man does before he decides to get married and settle down. It's the time when he is running around a lot.

"Mr. C.D.'s father was the overseer of a large plantation here and he acquired 10,000 acres. Mr. C.D. inherited the land as a young man, ran around for some years, then married me. We came here to settle down. We have three fine children, one boy and two girls, who are married."

Mrs. C.D. showed me their whole house, including their bedroom, bragging a bit that the maid and her husband came to the home at 3:30 a.m. each day in the fall and winter to light the bedroom fireplace, then the other fireplaces and begin breakfast. I wondered how the hell they could keep sleeping with people in the bedroom working. They did not seem to regard their help as people.

I was impressed that the couple owned more than 10,000 acres. I was from Wisconsin, where a 160-acre milk farm was considered plenty.

My thoughts returned to the people on the bus. I asked someone close to me, "Why don't people want to stop at C.D.'s store?"

"Oh my, Brother Keil, that's a long story. I don't think you want to know. Maybe Mose Thornton there could tell you one day."

Mose and I had become friendly working and swimming together. He was sitting across the aisle and listening to everything being said about Mr. C.D.

"Mose," I said. "Can you help me understand?"

He began softly, "You see my mother in the back of the bus? She told me once he killed her brother and another man. It was over an argument about how much they owed him. Mr. C.D. drinks a lot and gets mad and ugly."

I couldn't believe it. I just listened as Mose continued. "Mr. C.D. goes up to Phenix City and pays bail for some of the prisoners, and they come to work for him until they've paid him back. They may have to work six months or a year. If they don't do everything he says, he just calls the sheriff, who takes them back to jail.

"He and my uncle disagreed over money, and he killed him." And the law, he went on, decided Mr. C.D. did nothing wrong.

I didn't know what to say, whether to believe the man I met was capable of murder or not, whether to be mad or sad. Priests at Holy Trinity were friendly with Mr. C.D. Then I thought about the speaker and the goodness of the people on the bus. Mrs. Thornton, the sister of one of the victims, was not from an old storybook, nor did this take place 100 years ago. Mrs. Thornton was sitting in the back of the bus and her son, the nephew of one of the dead men, was telling me about the killing. It was another epiphany: Often there's one set of facts, figures and memories in the white community and a whole different set of facts, figures and memories in the black community. I learned that often the memories in the white community were selective.

We traveled more miles, then into Barbour County, home to several Alabama governors, including segregationist George Wallace from Clio. People wanted to stop at a little store to get drinks and other small things. We piled out of the bus, laughing, joking and beginning to relax and know one another. Someone had given me an RC Cola on the bus so I wasn't thirsty, but I went into the store anyway.

"No, we don't have bathrooms for niggers," the shopkeeper was saying as I came in. "God damn, do you want a Coke or RC? I don't have time to wait on you. ... Damn you kid, don't be putting your hands on those potato chips." All of this venom and trash was being spewed out, and we had come into this man's store to do business.

I looked toward the man behind the counter and he was scowling at me, wondering, I'm sure, what a white man was doing with this group. The elderly women in our group wandered outside to go to the bathroom in the bushes. I shuddered as I thought of the small children being exposed to hate and rejection so young, and the teens being denigrated at a time when they needed a little affirmation and acceptance.

I was beginning to be exposed to the real world that black people lived in every day. I was seeing a part of life I had never seen. I was being taught just who was civilized and who was not. I felt strange, but not afraid. I had to confront myself, my thoughts and feelings right away. If I felt ashamed to be with these black people in public, I might as well pack my bags and leave Alabama instead of living a fake, paternalistic life of service. No, by God, I was proud to be there with these lovely, strong people, I thought. To hell with what others think.

Thelma and Paul kept a watch over each person in the store and checked on the others who were relieving themselves in the bushes. As we all got on the bus, I felt the discomfort of the abuse. I began to talk about how crude the shopkeeper had been. I said to Paul, "Wasn't that terrible the way everyone was treated, with him using such terrible language and making people use the bushes for the bathroom?"

"Yes, Brother Keil, but we all are used to that and we learn to forget it and go on. We get what we need to get and try not to cause any trouble."

Thelma chimed in. "Brother Keil, those people are mean. But we are here on the bus, and I want to make sure we all have a good time today and not argue with people like that."

We spoke a while longer about what had happened. For Thelma and Paul, it was what they expected and they knew how to deal with it. I was listening and learning.

We stopped several more times to fix a flat tire, repair a boiling radiator, replenish the oil, get gas, colas and moon pies. We received the same stares, endured the same vile language and same lack of gratitude, even though we were spending money.

After each stop, we would all pile back on the bus. I would find out more about each person and his or her family. We finally arrived in Panama City, and Paul and Thelma consulted about where to go. I thought they were just looking for the beach. We continued to drive. After a few more miles and several turns here and there, they found the sign, "Colored Only." It had never even occurred to me that we couldn't just go to the closest beach.

We pulled into the parking area. The beach was so beautiful and the sand so white for miles and miles. The pale green waves were coming in with their white froth, and the sky was as blue as it could be. We all got off the bus, different small groups and families gathering together with their blankets, towels and food. Someone had brought a charcoal grill, and they set it up and got the fire going. A couple of teens took the tub of iced drinks off the bus and put it in a central location on the beach.

Some of us drifted toward the water, while many stayed on the shore. Most could not swim. Swimming wasn't a common form of recreation for blacks in rural Alabama. Chopping cotton, picking cotton, carrying water, washing clothes, washing dishes, cleaning toilets and cutting wood were the skills of survival. Eventually, many waded in, and I asked Mose and others to help me watch everyone as lifeguards would. The teenagers began to have fun splashing about. The grown-ups waded in cautiously, warning others not to splash or bother them.

This is terrific, I thought. We're the only people here. More people should know about this beach. The beaches of Lake Michigan and the lakes of Wisconsin and Minnesota are great, but not nearly as spectacular as this.

From a distance, I saw a pickup truck drive up and a black man get out and begin to walk toward me. I wondered who he might be. I waded out of the water and walked on the beach and saw he was in a park service truck. The man said, "Sir, I am sorry, but we do not allow white people on this beach. This is only for colored. You have to leave."

Everyone on the beach had stopped playing and was gathering around the park man and me. "This is a church group, and I am the chaperone," I said. "I can't leave without taking all of the others. We come from a little place north of Eufaula and south of Phenix City, Alabama. We come from such a distance that this is a once-a-year outing. Please, couldn't you let us stay?"

The man thought to himself and said, "Well, Sir, it's not that I have anything against it, but I have to ask my boss."

He drove off and a few minutes later, another truck drove up with another man. He was white. I greeted him politely.

He said, "I understand that you want to stay here. This isn't the way things are done here. I think you have to go."

Again, I gave my reason for wanting to stay. He was not unkind, but he was nervous. He gave me the same answer that the first man had given me. "I'm not against you staying, but I will have to ask my boss."

So off the second man went to his pickup truck and, 10 minutes later, another pickup truck with another man came driving up. He was white and a bit larger, with his park badge and hat on. He got out of the truck and slowly looked around and began to walk over to us, all now standing in a circle. Again, I said, "Hi, Sir."

He had been briefed about my conversations with the two other men and began by saying, "Son, now look here, we're not trying to cause you any trouble because we don't like trouble. I'll tell you what, if I don't get any complaints from anybody, I'll let y'all stay here. Just make sure you clean up the place when you leave and make sure there's no drinking."

"Thank you very much, Sir," I said. "We'll take good care of the place, and we don't have any alcohol." We shook hands, and we all thanked him again.

We were relieved and happy to be able to stay. I felt that the three men, in their way, were trying to be decent. The teens, young adults and elderly people were happy to have this episode over and to get back to being human and enjoying life. Little did we know when we left Holy Trinity that we were embarking on our own Freedom Ride and protesting in our own little way.

The hotdogs and hamburgers were ready, with potato salad, potato chips, RC Colas and moon pies. We ate, then played ball, ran, swam, walked, talked, laughed, splashed and wore ourselves out. In the late afternoon, Paul and Thelma began to round up everyone, saying we needed to head back to Holy Trinity. It would be late by the time we returned. We all got back on the bus after cleaning the grounds. No one else had come to this glorious beach the entire day. I didn't understand why, but I would learn on the way back home. People were still laughing and talking as our bus pulled out of the parking lot.

Thelma hushed everyone and did a count of all present, making sure we weren't leaving anyone. She again asked me to lead the group in a prayer for a safe and happy trip home. I first had to say, "Thank you all for a wonderful day." The people on the bus clapped, shouting, "Thank you, Brother Keil." I felt so good and proud of being a small part of their lives. Paul drove the bus out of the beach area to the highway leading back to Alabama.

"Brother Keil, I don't want to worry you, but I need to look at a tire and repair our radiator. Maybe we can find some jars of water to carry for the radiator. We need to stop at a garage."

"Whatever you think best, Paul," I responded. Although I began to worry if we would be treated like trash as we were on our trip down to the beach.

Paul said, "I think I can find a garage that will help us."

I didn't know what Paul knew. That is, in every little town we would pass through, there would be black people doing the work in garages owned by white folk or in garages of their own in humble buildings or under shade trees. They would help us. Sure enough, Paul found a garage, and a man fixed the radiator hose, gave us some extra bottles with water for the road and filled the tank with gas. It seemed like a long wait to everyone, now eager to get back home. But we were patient.

We started again, knowing we would need to stop a couple of times for restrooms that we couldn't use, to buy refreshments while being told to go to hell and listening to slurs. We settled down for the ride back, everyone talking quietly to those in the seats around them, except for a couple of teens who had fallen in love on the trip like teens all over the world. They had eyes only for each other. I wondered aloud, "Why were there no other people on the beach?"

Either Paul or Thelma explained, "Brother Keil, most colored people can't take off on a weekday to go to the beach. And, even if they could, most would not have a bus to take them there."

This all sounds so obvious to me now. But back then, it was a revelation. Paul kept driving, and I was amazed at his strength and sense of calm. He was pleasant to all, even after a long drive to Panama City and a day of playing in the sun. Even while driving the long road back to Holy Trinity with the bus straining at the seams. Thelma was her beautiful self, the person everyone turned to with their questions.

Our teen club's outing to Panama City had come at a time when, all over the country, the way blacks and whites interact was being challenged. And I was only just beginning to see the problems our country had to overcome.

CHAPTER 9

I WAS A CHANGED MAN when I came back to Loras College from Alabama.

The South had exposed me to the injustices and terrorism that black people faced on a daily basis. I made up my mind to dedicate my life to changing such conditions. It seemed to me that the Trinitarian order would offer the best chance of engaging in such work. Sure, Trinitarians had their problems. But at least they were out living among the poor. Besides, I didn't know much about other orders – Franciscans or Dominicans or Jesuits; and diocesan priests seemed far removed from the type of work I was now burning to do.

I filled out an application for acceptance into the Trinitarian seminary. My grades at Loras College and its seminary were very good. And, since I had spent a whole summer with the Trinitarians, they knew about me. I wasn't a shoo-in, but I felt confident. Father Norbert, who had been a great role model during my time at Holy Trinity, and Father Vogl, my spiritual director at Loras, were very good friends.

I was ecstatic when I was chosen. I felt that God was guiding me. In those days of many seminary applicants, I would have been turned down in a minute if there were any doubts. My teachers and fellow students at Loras were happy for me. My family wanted what was best for me, but really knew little about the priesthood, orders, the injustices in the South or the needs of the black community.

I started studying Dr. Martin Luther King Jr., Langston Hughes, W.E.B Dubois and the Morehouse College newsletter. I was privately gaining knowledge in subjects of which others in the seminary were hardly aware. I was young and infatuated with liberation issues. I was determined to make my life relevant.

I finished my second year at Loras and, in early June, went straight to Holy Trinity. Most seminarians were on break. I took classes in Greek and Latin the mornings, then worked the fields in the afternoon. At night, I studied. In the fall, the whole seminary came back.

It was a busy year, but I still found a little time to meet people in the surrounding communities.

Eliah Miles' tin-roof sharecropper cabin was down a dusty clay road off Highway 165, near Cottonton, Alabama. I came across him one brisk day while I was out walking. He was sweeping his yard with a broom, clearing sticks and debris so he could easily spot snakes. He had a scattered a perimeter of sulfur in an attempt to keep the vermin out.

It was about 9 a.m., but he was perspiring. The smell of the smoke coming from his chimney filled the air, and he had a nice size woodpile stacked up by the door of his cabin. His ax, sharp and shiny from recent use, leaned against the side of his house. Eliah looked up with his easy smile.

"Hi, Brother," the gray-haired man called. "How are you today? It sure is a sunny day, even though it is nippy. Would you like to come inside by the fire?"

What a generous offer, I thought. Here I am a stranger and this man invites me to come in and talk. Of course, he knew I was from the Catholic seminary; our land bordered the land he rented. I accepted his offer and went inside the cabin.

Old newspapers covered the cracks in the walls. The fire blazed and gave out an even heat.

"Brother, do you want something to eat?" he asked, gesturing toward a frying pan on the wood stove that still held some cornbread. "I cooked it myself. I do everything by myself. I mostly sit on the porch and read the Bible. I have to get my own wood, and I don't get around like I used to. The Bible says two times we become children, and it is true. I act like a child more each day. Lord, I forget so much."

"You seem to be doing great," I told him. "You take care of yourself, your home and your yard, chop wood and cook and clean. I hope to do that well for myself when I am your age."

Eliah, like so many others I had encountered, seemed to defy every stereotype. He was a hard-working man of God. He was generous and friendly, though he had no reason to believe a white man would return his kindness.

"Brother, let me tell you something. I have been around a long time. You heard tell of Mr. C.D.?" he asked.

"Yes, I heard of him." I was surprised that he even mentioned C.D.

"Mr. C.D. and I are the same age, about 80," he exclaimed with a bit of pride and caution. "We were born a few days apart, and my mother was his wet nurse. She worked for his daddy and momma. They had a lot of land. C.D. grew up but wasn't of much account until he married. She came from Texas."

"I heard that sometimes Mr. C.D. is not very nice," I guardedly said.

Eliah laughed a bit and said, "Oh, he ain't that bad. He has always been good to me. I give him a bale of cotton each year for living in this house. I buy at his store and, if I don't have money, he lets me borrow from him."

I said that I had heard that he had shot a couple of people over debts.

"Well, Brother," Eliah said, clearly not comfortable discussing any of C.D.'s transgressions with me, "God will judge all of us, and I try to live peaceably with all God's children." With that, Eliah ended the conversation on C.D. and moved on to another subject.

We visited for a little while longer, then I left. I would occasionally stop by on future walks, just to check in. Eliah was always nice, but he kept the boundaries he was taught. No matter how much I wanted to rush things, I found, it takes a while to build trust, and black people had everything to lose by trusting the wrong person. These were volatile times.

I always admired how Eliah, at such an advanced age, managed to keep up his cabin and take care of himself. He always seemed to have words of wisdom for me. I was thankful Eliah took the time to talk, to welcome me to the area.

At Holy Trinity, I found the seminary quite different from Loras. I enjoyed little of the independence I did there. Sometimes, the Trinitarian priests treated us seminarians as if we were children. They had little use for our opinions.

We were taught that we needed to be dependent on superiors and professors. In fact, outside of our studies, we were discouraged from using our own judgment. I could only hope life would improve once I became a full-fledged priest.

Before long, our seminarian class was sent for a stint in Brackney, Pennsylvania, where the order had a farm and a religious house next to a beautiful lake. It was a large place, housing 12 seminarians, two priests and a religious brother. The seminarians slept two in a room.

We all had to choose another name. For the most part, this is what we would be called from then on, except by a few people close to us, who might slip and refer to us by our given names. This signified that we were leaving our old selves behind and becoming new and better. There are big elaborate books with many saints' names and their derivations. I chose my father's name, Emil. I had much respect for my father. He was a good, loving, hard-working man. I could do no better. This made my father proud.

Of course, I had very little contact with my family, not even on the phone. In many ways, I was very lonely. But, with

God's guidance and help, I tried to keep my mind on my goal. And I looked forward to the time when I would return to the South.

CHAPTER 10

I WAS STANDING ON A blistering hot sidewalk when Father August introduced me to a tall, brown-haired man. It was not long after Phenix City, Alabama, known far and wide for its crime and corruption, had been cleaned up. "This is Jack Miller from Phenix City," Father August said.

Little did I know that, over the course of years, Jack and I would become the best of friends. I had great admiration for Jack. Though we thought differently on many issues, we accepted and loved one another.

Jack had been a Marine fighter pilot in World War II, flying P38s in the South Pacific. He lied about his age and went into the service when he was 17. He served bravely and honorably, but never cottoned to the structure. A commander in the South Pacific told him one day, "Miller, you came into this outfit a lieutenant, and I promise you that you will leave a lieutenant."

He had little care about moving up in rank.

The war ended, and Jack was off to law school with the likes of future Alabama Gov. George Wallace. Afterward, Jack was an FBI agent for a few years, then came home to practice law in Phenix City.

His law partner, John Patterson, was Alabama's attorney general and would go on to become the governor, known for defending segregation laws. Patterson's father, Albert, had been murdered in the 1950s, while running for state attorney general, campaigning on the promised of ridding the city of vice.

Because Jack did some work for Holy Trinity, I saw him often. We had both been in the military, so we had that in common. His father had owned a tire shop. We started eating lunch together regularly. I learned much about him. Jack was a son of the South and shared many of the opinions on race relationships that other whites in the area had. He viewed blacks as generally untrustworthy. But, like many others, he was conflicted. He could see and identify with the humanity of black people on an individual basis, but tended to stereotype the race.

I explained to Jack why I enjoyed working in the black community at Holy Trinity and told him how prejudice made the lives of good people so hard. I did not feel compelled to preach to him, but I was clear about where I stood. Still we discussed the subject often. I wanted to understand what he and others thought; I wanted to understand what the obstacles were to better race relations. Jack would kindly answer my questions, trying to explain how he and others were raised. He also asked questions.

Jack went on to become a circuit court judge in Phenix City. He said he worked to overcome his prejudice. Only he knows how successful he was.

Knowing him to be a smart, kind man, though flawed, I tried to avoid making harsh generalizations about white southerners.

Jack often told me stories about his life, one that happened when he was a young man in college. He was digging a ditch with an elderly black man at his father's tire shop. It began to rain, and an irritated Jack started to curse and carry on. The man stopped and said, "Mr. Miller, how old are you?"

Caught off guard by the question, Jack quickly muttered, "I'm 18."

To this, the elderly man said, "Well, Mr. Miller, if the Lord has put up with you for 18 years, through thick and thin, surely you can put up with his rain for a few minutes."

Jack said that he stopped and thought about his impatience and crude impulses. He thought about how he had gotten flustered by a relatively minor event, whereas the man working with him just continued digging, unbothered and undeterred. It was a lesson he said he never forgot: Don't sweat the small stuff. And in that moment, he said, his teacher seemed as wise as any he'd ever had.

CHAPTER 11

I HARDLY EVER FELT LIKE myself, it seemed.

Studying for the Trinitarian order, I began to notice that depression and anxiety were becoming a part of my everyday life. While I loved the time I spent out in the community, life in the order was regimented and stressful. I felt isolated, though I was surrounded by people. I tried to pay little attention to these nagging feelings. The reason for my depression and anxiety, I thought, was clear: I just didn't measure up to the other priests and brothers in the order. Everyone else seemed so pious, so sure of himself – or so drunk.

Booze was ever present in religious life, I was learning. Maybe it stemmed from the pressure some felt to be perfect at all times, or the smothering effect of the Church's authoritarian structure, or the loneliness of having no significant other. Whatever the reason, the problem was obvious.

The religion teacher drank profusely. He was pitiful really. He seemed to want to hide his slim body, receding hairline and effeminate ways. He was the choirmaster and full of guilt, shame and anger. He would yell at us if he thought we weren't singing a song correctly, then feel remorseful. His red and purple face, along with his many visits to the doctor, earned him the name "The Kidney" from the other seminarians.

The alcoholic speech teacher was a gruff, stocky man who wore his black biretta cocked on his head as he swaggered into a room. He would try to teach us public reading, but occasionally would go off on drunken tirades.

"I don't know why in the hell you can't read clearer! The words are on the page! Goddamn, read them loud and read them again.

"And you want to be a priest? Jesus!" he would shout and roll his eyes.

Despite the bullying, we tried to learn and feel the presence of God. Father Elliot, the college prefect, advised us all to meditate a half hour each day on the writings of the founder of the Trinitarians, Father Thomas Augustine Judge. I did not even know how to meditate. I would watch the priests and brothers during the designated meditation time, hoping to pick up some pointers. At first, it looked as though Father Elliot and some of the other priests and brothers were in ecstasy, with their heads bobbing back and forth, until I noticed they were actually dozing off.

The sermons and studies taught us that we should not have "dirty" thoughts, and we were not to masturbate. These were grievous mortal sins and must be confessed to a priest before going to communion each morning. We had to be sorry for such sins and promise not to commit them again.

I felt guilty and ashamed for masturbating on occasion. I was a very bad person, hardly worthy of the priesthood.

With all the mental and emotional strain, my studies began to suffer, and I failed some Religious and Greek tests, even though I had been an A student at Loras College. I also began to struggle with Latin.

Father Flynn insisted that Latin was a divine language, that it was God's law and the Church's law that we study in Latin. The Cardinal who headed the Holy Office in Rome issued a decree stating this as a divine preference. I did not know the Cardinal or anything about the Holy Office. But I did know that the first Latin Bibles were translations from other languages, so it seemed to me that God got along without Latin for a long time.

I can hear his words now in class, "Why can't you translate the passage? I just cannot pass you if you can't make the grade."

I told him most students in the class were using "ponies," that is, English translations of the Latin. Using ponies to translate had been considered cheating at Loras College. I felt ashamed, like a dumb ass, but I couldn't use a pony in good conscience.

All of the harsh criticism was the daily, accepted way of life. I had two years of overseas duty in the Army and had not witnessed such sick, erratic behavior even there. But I was not a quitter.

I added activities to my routine that I had always enjoyed in the past, like playing sports. But in the seminary, I participated with little enthusiasm and average performance.

Though I felt tired all the time, I kept studying black history and sociology on the side, along with the lives of the saints, history and theology. At mealtimes, the seminarians talked and laughed, sitting next to the same people year after year, under the watchful eyes of the same priests.

There were classes and pastimes that I enjoyed. I loved studying Canon Law. I loved my job as the seminary plumber, fixing clogged toilets, leaky sinks, broken showers and cracked radiators, and I loved being the driver the superiors would call on to transport other seminarians or priests. I loved my walks with other seminarians.

Then, I would pretend we actually were leaving the seminary grounds and going somewhere else. We would talk along the way and discuss whatever we wanted, without the priests in charge judging us.

I remembered hearing the shouts and laughter of the guys and girls coming from the autumn football games when I was at Loras, up in my room studying Chemistry or Latin. I was sure then that I would one day feel my sacrifices were all worth it. Now, the memory just made me feel sad. I knew that I could not be with a woman again. Sometimes I cried, even though I had not dated many.

I still felt that I wanted to sacrifice and dedicate my life to God as a celibate priest. But, at Loras College, I had felt valued by the seminary authorities and professors. Studying for the priesthood among the Trinitarians, I felt the opposite. It seemed to me that some of those in charge considered me ignorant and unworthy of the vocation.

For the next eight years, I would study and labor under these feelings, but I endured. I made up my mind that I was going to serve God. I was going to be a priest. I was going do my part to make a difference in this world.

CHAPTER 12

ONCE, THE NORTHWEST PART OF Washington, D.C., was white and moneyed. By the early 1960s, however, it was black and poor.

Urban poverty was different from the kind that existed in the rural South. In D.C., adding to the economic despair was violence, burglaries, trash in the streets and a general lack of services. The poor in Alabama had little but shared more of a sense of community. Even those who had no money could find a plot of land to grow food. When the bitter cold set in, they could chop wood for fire.

The Trinitarians ran Fides Neighborhood House at 8th and Q streets. Monsignor Paul Hanly Furfey of Catholic University had founded Fides House in the '50s. It offered social and recreational services to the neighborhood.

My work there and out in the community gave me a fresh outlook and helped me change my mental disposition. I was filled with joy teaching and watching over children at the house. My walk home every night around 9 p.m. was a highlight of my day. All along the way, people would be sitting on their front stoops, trying to escape stifling hot apartments. Children would play in the streets. As I walked in the dark, I would hear friendly greetings from parents and children – "Hi, Brother!" "Good evening, Brother!" I would return the greeting and sometimes pause to talk.

I was a lucky man. I went home to air conditioning and a supper of some sort. And my day always began with breakfast. I had once foolishly assumed regular meals were part of everyone's life – at least in America. I was mistaken.

At Fides House, I was in charge of 20 little 7 year olds. We had classes in the morning, and played, sang and ate together. One afternoon, our little group was in the park on the swings and merry-go-rounds when little Susan came running up to me, tears flowing down her face. "Brother, come real quick! Ron Washington hit Mary and another girl with a stick, over by the swings."

More than likely, this was an overreaction by Susan, I first thought. But when I got closer, I saw large fresh welts on the girls' shoulders and chests. They continued to cry as I held them, then one of the women of the park service took them to a faucet to wash their welts with cold water. I went to find Ron.

"Ron, did you hit those girls?"

He looked frightened. "Brother, they wouldn't give me part of their lunch, and I didn't have any."

"Why didn't you have your lunch? Your parents are supposed to send lunch with you every day. Don't tell me that you didn't have lunch."

"No, Brother," he said, beginning to cry. "My momma told me that we had no food today, and we had no food yesterday."

"I don't believe you. Don't you ever think you can hit another child, especially those girls." Angry and frustrated, I slapped his face. Catholic schools are supposed to lay down the law, I said to myself. I simply didn't believe what this kid was telling me, that he hadn't had food for two days.

"Ron, what is your mother's phone number and when will she be home?"

The boy told me the number and said his mother was usually at home nights.

I called her that evening. "Mrs. Washington, your son, Ron, hit two little girls with a stick today. He said it was because they would not share their lunches and that he hadn't eaten today or yesterday. I hit him for telling me such lies."

"Brother, I am sorry that Ron hit the girls, and I punished him when I found out about it when he came home today. He knows better than to hit other children, and I'm so sorry. But, Brother, he didn't lie about the food. We've had no food for these past two days."

I said something more to her, but I was too surprised to remember what. I hung up the phone and cried. Ron hadn't lied. He hadn't eaten for two days. I was so damned righteous and such a know-it-all. Later as a priest, I decided not to allow corporal punishment in the schools I headed. I learned the hard way.

Fides House immediately helped Ron's family get groceries, not just that week, but for many weeks.

At Fides, we often took the children on outings. I would drive our yellow school bus filled with enthusiastic children and their equally energized counselors. Parents also frequently came along. We went to the city's parks, museums, government buildings and nearby Carr's Beach and Sparrow's Beach on the Chesapeake. The two segregated black beaches near Annapolis provided a wonderful place for black families to gather, relax and picnic.

The parents often talked about injustices they suffered, and I listened with interest. Not all of their stories were of bad times. We also talked about family dreams and accomplishments over Kool-Aid and sandwiches.

I was often the only white guy among hundreds of African Americans on these vast beaches. We would locate a place to put our towels, blankets and food, then some of the children and I would head toward the water.

Carr's Beach was on the "Chitlin Circuit." Each week a different band or musical group played at the beach: The Drifters, Little Richard, The Coasters, the Shirelles and a long line of the top stars of the '50s. I would often spend time talking to the musicians during their intermissions. I knew these entertainers were popular, but I had no idea just how popular or of their impact on the musical world.

The Shirelles formed one of the first all-girl bands, and their biggest hit, "Will You Love Me Tomorrow?" became the first No. 1 single in the rock era by an all-girl group. Doris Coley of the Shirelles and I talked before and after the concerts. I also got a chance to talk to members of the Coasters, who had the hit "Poison Ivy." Musicians from both groups would speak of filthy dressing rooms and segregated venues, even though their groups were at the top of the music charts.

Patricia Price, a teen who frequented our Neighborhood House and participated in many of our programs, came to me one day after she saw me speaking with Doris of the Shirelles.

"Brother, would you ask her if I could talk to her about becoming a singer?"

Since Doris was only 20 yards away and on break, I suggested that she speak to the singer herself.

"Really?"

I smiled and said, "Yes."

Patricia walked over to her, and they talked. After a while she came back, as happy as she could be. I was eager to know what had been said. "She was so very nice," Patricia gushed.

"She even asked me to sing for her, and she said I had a very good voice. Then she asked me to promise that I would first go to college to study music before I became a singer. She said that the performing she did was very hard because she had to use dirty dressing rooms, stay in run-down segregated hotels and eat in segregated restaurants. She said that, even though she made good money, most of it went to the producers, managers and the tax man." A good education, Doris told Patricia, would help in managing a musical career.

I often wished that other whites could have been with me on those beaches, crowded with people laughing and having fun, sometimes discussing the issues of the day. Had they been, they may have been able to understand the impact of segregation and injustices. They may have been able to see the pride, the goodness, the beauty and the strength so evident in the African-American community. And it would have been great for them to experience being a minority, one among hundreds of African Americans. Then maybe they would learn to be at ease around those different from themselves and to leave their fears and ignorance at the door.

I learned much about community organizing during my time in D.C., from parents, volunteers, government workers, educators and activists, like Mary Houston, director of Fides House.

She was one of the rarest of people during those times: She was white, but had genuine love for the black community and was dedicated to working to improve race relations. She understood that churches had a responsibility to try to change the cultural and economic structures that contributed to social ills and poverty.

Mary was my mentor and guide. She was somewhat older than I and extremely focused. Philosophically, she could have been the younger sister of Dorothy Day, the renowned social leader who helped found the Catholic Worker movement. I often asked myself what went into making Mary such a lovely, intelligent and capable leader.

Sometimes, Mary would call the three of us brothers into her office to review how the summer was going at Fides. She often would praise us, but had no problem chastising. "Brothers," she would say, "I've been noticing too much fooling around by you before classes in the mornings. I want you to get focused right away. The children come here to learn. Their parents send them to us to learn. I expect you to teach them, beginning now!"

Mary was forthright and never defensive. She smiled freely and loved the folks in the neighborhood. She never made fun of people or talked behind their backs. She wasn't preachy but commanded respect.

After I had left, I did not see or talk to her for five years, but frequently drew inspiration from her and tried to follow her example. Then I ran into her at Catholic University. We greeted one another warmly, and she told me she had left her job at Fides House to take a position at the Archdiocese.

Even with some gray hair, she still looked young and beautiful. We talked for a while, then she asked, "Richard, would you consider being my spiritual director while I'm at Catholic University?"

I was flattered. Here this wonderfully gifted person was asking *me* to play such an important role in her life. It was a much-needed affirmation after all the negative feedback I had received at the seminary. Of all the priests she knew in Washington and at Catholic University, she was asking me. I quickly agreed.

We met on several occasions, and it became obvious that she didn't feel fulfilled pursuing her doctorate. She wanted to get back to hands-on work.

We talked many hours. She had taken personal vows of poverty, chastity and obedience without ever joining a religious order. Almost no one knew of her profound religious and spiritual depth.

I grew tremendously listening to her talk as she tried to discern what God wanted for her life. She was willing to delay her short-term happiness in the interest of her long-term goal of serving the community. Mary finished her doctorate in social work and went back to the Archdiocese to put it to use.

Four years later, I was in rural Alabama when I received a letter from a friend telling me that Mary had died of cancer. I was sad and shaken to think that my friend and mentor, so determined to make a difference, had left this world at such a young age.

CHAPTER 13

I<small>N MANY WAYS, THE SEMINARY</small> was similar to the Army, except the hours were longer. That became especially true in the autumn of 1960, when our class was sent from the main Trinitarian seminary in Winchester, Virginia, back to Alabama to study philosophy for a year.

I looked forward to going back to a community so familiar, back to friends and parishioners who had been so good to me. Father Fabian would be our Master of Clerics, the priest in charge of every aspect of seminarian life. He was tall and husky. In the classroom, he would often digress from the Latin philosophy book and give us his take on life or expound on the lessons to be learned from the Peanuts character Snoopy. Unlike some who found themselves in authority, he was kind and patient with us. And we were grateful.

I would get up at 4 a.m., make a coal fire, take milk to Brother Pierre, who had ulcer problems, and wait until the

5:30 a.m. bell for morning prayers. On Sunday mornings, seminarians would rise around 6 a.m. for prayers, meditation and Mass as usual. At 9 a.m., we would hold a Solemn High Mass.

The other seminarians had begun to complain about the cold as winter approached. Clearly, our heating wasn't adequate. I asked Father Fabian if I could install steam heat in our dormitories, and he consented. These do-it-yourself projects kept my spirits up. Though I had never done anything like it, I approached the project with glee. I appreciated the challenge.

After my daily classes were finished, I would use some of my study time to work on the heating system. As I look back on it, I'm proud that I could pass my studies and still do this additional work.

Though I had looked forward to returning to Holy Trinity and looking up friends, the seminary's stringent rules meant I had little or no contact with people on the outside. So I took a chance and asked Father Fabian for permission to go to the 11 a.m. Mass, where Thelma, Paul, Esau and others might be in attendance.

Knocking at his door at the end of the long wooden dorm building, I heard him say, "Come in."

I opened the door and, acting like the nervous child that the seminary turns a man into, blurted out my request. "Hi,

Father Fabian. May I go to the 11 a.m. Mass at the mission? I will come back right after."

Father Fabian was easy going, even though his actions were dictated by an unyielding set of rules, rules he had to follow and see that we followed, too. "Yes, Brother," he said. "But don't be late. We have vespers, compline and benediction at 1:30. Father Robert, Father Francis and Father Willis will be looking for everyone then."

I was truly grateful. I walked down to the mission. Mass had already started, and the priest was going up the aisle with the people singing the entrance hymn. I found a seat in the back of the small church. Smiles were everywhere, and I was thrilled to be there.

After Mass, we all piled out of church and began our hugs and greetings. I felt like I was home again, catching up on all the news, meeting new wives and husbands and children, hearing about new jobs, new hopes, new dreams. Thelma was going to have her first child. Paul Anthony had married. I was introduced to the nuns now teaching at the school.

I could tell instantly that my friends loved these sisters, and, in return, the sisters loved them. The sisters could tell I loved the parishioners there, too. The usual boundaries that often separate people in and out of religious life broke down.

The principal of the mission school, Sister Ann Bernard, and I became instant friends. She asked Father Fabian if I could be allowed to come speak to a 7th and 8th grade religion class. I ran into her again after a Christmas Mass. We spoke briefly, and I noticed her dark hair, beauty and dedication. She had a serious nature, but I could easily bring a smile to her lovely face. We weren't interested in each other in a romantic way. We knew the rules. But there was solidarity there.

As the principal of a school in poor, rural Alabama, Sister Ann Bernard felt heavy burdens, given the school's overwhelming needs and the lack of support. She knew that the order's fund-raising efforts brought in money in the name of the poor, but not enough was invested in the school.

Over the course of time, she revamped the school into a truly great place by demanding much of the faculty, the children, the parents and all associated with the mission. She decided to hire lay teachers from the area, Thelma being the first one.

It's difficult to describe my friendship with Sister Ann Bernard. We didn't see each other much, but she was an inspiration. Sister was not afraid to get close to her students and their parents. Some thought she got too close, but she didn't let those criticisms bother her. She trusted her own instincts, even though religious life often discourages such self-reliance. She was encouraging to the teachers in the school, both religious and lay.

Ann Bernard left Holy Trinity a few years after we met, tired of the lack of cooperation from the order, but she remained a sister and was assigned to a northern parish.

I would like to tell you that the end of this story is not sad, but it is. Years later, when I was ordained a priest, I requested to go to Philadelphia to visit her on her deathbed. She was roughly 35 but eaten up with cancer. I was shown to her room in the infirmary at the Motherhouse on Solly Avenue. Her complexion was pale, face gaunt, lips parched, little left to her body. I prayed with her, not really knowing what to do in the face of death.

I would be in this situation many times in the future as a priest, but then I had little experience. And this was a beloved friend, one who had unselfishly lived the Gospel, serving others every day. The Sister Ann Bernard in front of me was so sick and in terrible pain. Tears came to my eyes as I stood in her room.

Driving out of Philadelphia, I openly sobbed. It all seemed so unfair. Sister Ann Bernard had given more in her short 10 to 15 years as a nun than many do in 50. I hoped that my life would be as meaningful.

For me, nuns were frequently sources of inspiration. I often was in awe of their dedication, endless energy and their capacity for forgiveness.

In the summer of 1964, I received permission to drive to the Motherhouse of the Oblate Sisters of Providence in Baltimore. A friend, Sister Julie, was making her first vows and had invited me to attend. The religious congregation was made up of only black sisters. They were about 500 strong and were primarily teachers. At the time, many other Catholic religious orders would neither welcome nor accept black sisters into their congregations. As unbelievable as it seems now, this was an accepted way of life in the Church. I have always struggled with the Church's hypocrisy in this regard.

Sister Julie and I had worked together in Washington, D.C. I was also friendly with her mother and father. Her goodness was infectious.

Because I was a seminarian, I was required to travel with another brother, so I asked Patrick Liteky to accompany me. Pat and I got along well and had fun talking and laughing all the way to Baltimore.

The Oblate Sisters' Motherhouse sat on a tall bluff. The day was beautiful with the sun shining on the multicolored flowers, the freshly cut grass and the green shrubbery.

Outside, there were long tables covered with linens, cold drinks, snacks and a variety of desserts. Several hundred people gathered as the newly professed sisters smiled and visited with family and guests. Many sisters who had professed years before milled around the crowd. It was a joyous occasion.

Sister Julie approached me, and we hugged. "Brother Emil, it is so great to see you! Thanks for coming."

"It's wonderful to see you," I said. "I'm so proud of you, Sister Julie."

"Do you remember when we walked the streets of Northwest D.C.?" Sister Julie asked. "We sure had a great time with the kids and parents at Fides, Banneker Pool and on the field trips on the bus."

Just then, her parents came up, and we hugged. They introduced Father Perry, the Provincial of the Society of Divine Word Fathers in Pass Christian, Mississippi. Sister Julie's mother said, "Father Perry is staying with us. We are old friends, and he always visits when he is in Washington."

I said, "It's an honor to meet you, Father Perry."

We talked for a few minutes before they continued on. Before he walked away, Father Perry said, "If you are ever in Mississippi, please come to see me."

Little did I know that, about a year later, I would be in Bay St. Louis, visiting Father Perry, a future bishop.

As Sister Julie's parents and Father Perry left, another sister came up to us. Sister Julie introduced us. "Sister Joetta, this is my friend I told you about, Brother Emil. Brother Emil, this is Sister Joetta, the treasurer general of the Oblate Sisters of Providence."

Sister Joetta had an air of seriousness.

I greeted her cheerfully and remarked, "I am so glad that Sister Julie has become an Oblate Sister of Providence."

"Naturally she became an Oblate sister. What else would she become?" Sister Joetta responded dryly.

"Well," I said, a little taken aback, "she could have become a Franciscan, Dominican, or Sister of Charity or some other kind of sister. I'm happy she's here."

She responded, "She is black, and we are an all-black religious order. Here, she will feel both challenged and accepted. The other orders will not be able to give her that. For all these years, most orders have refused to accept black candidates. They give a hundred excuses. And I know from the treatment our sisters often receive from other religious orders that they are either uncomfortable with us or just don't care to know us. They are often proud of what we do from a distance, just so long as we stay in our place. With the exception of a very few orders, they do not care to serve in the black community. There are just one or two rare exceptions. Trust me, I know."

I felt Sister was harsh. But, she was a friend of Sister Julie and a treasurer general of a religious order, so I listened. I wanted to know her thoughts about race and the Church. I continued asking questions. Sister Joetta was not shy about answering. This was a rare opportunity to learn firsthand.

As the crowd dispersed, we continued to talk.

"Brother Emil, since I was 8 in Kentucky, I always wanted to become a Catholic. My parents discouraged me from joining the Church, but allowed me to attend Mass on Sunday. There, I was allowed to sit in the back pew with a couple of other black people. When I was about 14, I wanted to become a sister. But, as I was not a Catholic and still very young, my parents and the priests asked me to hold off until I was 21.

"When I did become 21, I joined the Church and was told to wait two years before becoming a sister. I finally began to look for a religious order, and I knew I had only two choices. I could become an Oblate Sister of Providence in Baltimore or a Holy Family sister in New Orleans. These were the only two religious orders that freely accepted black sisters. I knew I would never go farther south, so I chose the Oblate Sisters.

"Now," she continued, "I have become the treasurer general of our sisters. I have to find funds for everything for these 500 sisters. We take care of travel, food, clothes, health, education and dozens of other needs. Yes, many of them get small salaries from teaching, but we go to very poor parishes that can hardly afford to have us. Most religious orders have sisters from wealthy or well-off families who help their religious orders. Most of our sisters came from poor families, and we cannot depend on endowments, gifts from estates or wealthy families in our schools."

I said, "Sister, how did you prepare for such a job? I'm a Trinitarian, and they have a large staff and solicit money from all over the United States. Have you ever heard of or talked to Father Gilbert of our congregation? Do you connect with other treasurer generals of other orders?"

Sister Joetta said she had studied finance and management since being appointed. Not a year went by that she didn't go to a business, development or management school.

"I have talked to Father Gilbert, and he has been very helpful, more than other sisters' congregations. I have struggled hard with the sisters. I go to their national conventions of treasurer generals, and I have to stay at a hotel apart from where they stay and meet. I often have to eat in other restaurants or hotels."

I felt the depth of her pain and saw the tears beginning to well up in her eyes. Even though she was somewhat older than I, I knew we would be friends for a long time.

Over the years, I sometimes drove up to the Oblate Sisters Motherhouse and stayed there overnight visiting Sister Julie, Sister Joetta and the other sisters there. In addition to having a wonderful visit, I came to better understand race relations within the Church. I eventually lost touch with Sister Joetta, but she is another example of a great teacher who entered my life and offered a glimpse into a world unknown to me. She helped me to understand how isolated black sisters felt. And she showed me that, despite those feeling, the sisters managed to survive emotionally by leaning on each other and God.

Lessons from the Priesthood

CHAPTER 14

ORDINATION DAY CAME ON JUNE 1, 1965. I was prostrate with my classmates at Sacred Heart Church in Winchester, while the other seminarians and priests were chanting the Litany of the Saints:

> LORD, have mercy on us.
> CHRIST, have mercy on us.
> LORD, have mercy on us.
> CHRIST, hear us.
> CHRIST, graciously hear us.
> GOD, THE FATHER OF HEAVEN, have mercy on us.
> GOD THE SON, REDEEMER OF THE WORLD, have mercy on us.
> GOD THE HOLY GHOST, have mercy on us.
> HOLY TRINITY, ONE GOD, have mercy on us...

It's a beautiful prayer, one of the oldest in the Church, and on and on it went. It was hot and humid in the packed church, which had no air conditioning. We wore our long white vestments for the three-hour service. Sweat was rolling off everyone, including the stately gray-haired Bishop of Richmond. As I was lying on the marble floor, many feelings washed over me. I was so glad, so relieved, to finally get to this moment.

My mother and father were there, as well as two of my sisters, Mary and Joyce. I still have the picture of us after the service, my father in the only suit he owned. My parents were so proud.

I looked forward to being a priest, to leaving behind the difficult life of a seminarian. The difference between the two was a gulf wider than an ocean. A priest is often treated as if he knows everything, at least by parishioners, while the order treats a seminarian as if he knows nothing. Now, 32 years old and ordained, I would not have to ask for toothpaste. I would not be forced to turn off my light at 9:30 p.m. Now I could even call my parents or brothers and sisters whenever I wanted. For 10 years, I could not.

I felt revived and looked forward to my new life as a priest.

The letter, from Father Gerard Fredericks, Custodian General, Missionary Servants of the Most Holy Trinity, began:

Dear Father Emil Keil, M.S.SS.T:

May the Grace and Peace of the Holy Spirit be with us forever. After prayer and counsel of the General Council, it seems to be the will of God that you report to Our Lady of Good Hope Church, DeLisle, Mississippi, for the summer and report to Trinitarian House, 503 Rock Creek Church Road, NW, August 15th to attend Catholic University until the summer of 1966.

These were my marching orders for the next year. I had never heard of DeLisle, but I didn't second guess the assignment. The rules were that you did what the custodian general told you to do. Besides, I wanted to go to a parish in the South. I knew enough about Mississippi to know that it would be a challenge, but this was why I had studied and labored for 10 years.

It was a hot, muggy day when I arrived in New Orleans. A short, chubby, graying priest greeted me with a low and somber voice.

"Hi, Father Emil. I'm Father Hubert." His face was reddish, but not from drink. His suit and black clerical front had food stains.

"Thank you, Father," I replied. "It is very good of you to pick me up."

"I had some stops to make in New Orleans anyway, and it was convenient," he said. "After we've finished with the errands, we can drive to DeLisle and get you settled."

It was my first time in New Orleans, a city that intrigues so many. But I didn't pay much attention; my mind was on my new summer assignment. After Father Hubert made all of his stops, he finally turned the car east, in the direction of Mississippi.

Mississippi was receiving a lot of national attention because of frightening, deadly happenings. Segregationists were trying to keep their kingdom, and the African-American community was struggling to assert its power. The summer before, James Chaney, Andrew Goodman and Michael Schwerner, three young civil rights workers who had been registering blacks to vote, were murdered in Neshoba County. At the time, 45 percent of Mississippi's population was black, but less than 5 percent was registered to vote.

I knew I wanted to participate in the civil rights struggle; in what capacity, I didn't know. I planned to connect with black leaders and take my cue from them. I would be there for only three months, but I would listen and learn.

Southern Mississippi is heavily Catholic from early Spanish and French settlements. The Trinitarians had 19 priests serving in different parishes in different parts of the state. In seminary, we heard from a number of these priests. Some would describe their work as fulfilling and meaningful; some would lament the fact that they were in Mississippi during such volatile times.

The farther away we got from New Orleans, the more the homes began to look ramshackle, the more the highway was littered with trash. Then we were in beautiful bayou country, with its serene water, large oaks and Spanish moss. Soon, we arrived at Our Lady of Good Hope, a quiet little church on the edge of DeLisle.

After I was shown my room, it was suppertime. I was introduced to Mela Duvier, the housekeeper, a youngish black woman who was outspoken but knew what to say, and what not to say, in the presence of white folk. She should have been running the parish instead of being a housekeeper. She had more sense than some priests and was more sober than many.

The supper atmosphere was casual with Father Hubert and Father Mike talking with Mela about church issues as she served supper. Mela was a Catholic and went to the black Catholic church. The church I was assigned to, it turned out, was all white. That was not at all what I expected. My religious order's mission was, in part, to serve the African-American community. I decided I would try to make the best of the situation and learn what I could.

Priests at the church in DeLisle covered several churches, including St. Ann in the Dubuisson community, the church that P.D. Ladner attended. P.D. was the name given him by the seminarians who taught religion at the church on Sundays. P.D. had three pretty daughters, hence the nickname.

I became good friends with P.D. and his family. P.D. was 6 feet 4 inches and weighed upward of 380 pounds. His stomach was immense. On hot Sunday afternoons at his house, he would lay half-naked in the middle of the floor with his mountainous stomach aimed at the ceiling, a little fan trying to cool him off.

"Did you know, Father," he said, "one day I had a bug itch on my back and it wouldn't go away, so I went to the doctor. He took a. 22 bullet out of my back. I guess it was a stray bullet that I got when I was driving the road scraper."

It seemed incredible to me that this fellow would be walking around with a bullet in him, thinking it was a mosquito bite.

"Father, let me tell you. We like the colored folks around here. They used to come to our church. Then, one day, we built a new church, and the Bishop came for the dedication. There wasn't enough room for the colored and whites, so the Bishop asked someone to announce to the church all the niggers should leave to give room for the whites. The colored never came back. They began their own church and got the Bishop to get an order priest for them."

I just listened, amazed at the racism and lack of awareness.

Culturally, southern Mississippi, with its laissez faire attitude, was much different from Alabama. In the rectory, there were two slot machines. One took nickels, and one took quarters. People would come by the rectory just to put money into the machines, donated by a Mr. Dubuisson, a county commissioner, parishioner and entrepreneur.

Father Hubert would empty the machines on occasion to help fund parish projects.

The parish also socked away the change given in Sunday collections to use on this and that. Father Hubert would keep the change in a couple of buckets in his closet. By not reporting that money, it lowered the amount taxed by the Bishop.

Sometimes the Irish Travelers would come by our church. I heard that they came from the Carolinas and lived like gypsies. They would paint homes, tar roofs or sell rolls of linoleum for kitchen and bathroom floors. Some people said the paint was cheap, the roofs still leaked, and the linoleum cracked.

They had unusual practices, which some priests seemed to encourage.

"Here, Father, bless my daughter that she may get married. She is 12."

"Father, bless my daughter that she may have a baby. She is married and is 14."

"Hey, Father, bless my 16-year-old son that he might find a nice wife."

"Father, here is some money for blessing my children."

The Travelers did not mix much with the other parishioners; they slept in trailers in the churchyard and used portable grills to cook. They invited me to eat with them and told stories. It was a joyful, interesting experience for me until the racial jokes started. I could not believe my ears, how harsh the language was toward black people, coming from another ethnic group that was widely discriminated against. I listened, questioned their assumptions about African Americans and tried not to get riled up. I wanted to encourage dialogue.

The toxic racial atmosphere and the violence that resulted from it had a serious effect on some white people, including priests. I would visit a fellow priest who had been assigned to Jackson, Mississippi, in 1963, the year Medgar Evers was shot down. The priest suffered a nervous breakdown, partly from the trauma of it all. Race seemed to permeate every aspect of life, and he just didn't have the temperament to deal with it.

Others were oddly unaffected. I was stunned by many priests' thinking on issues of race. I sometimes challenged them, knowing God was with me. I felt they were cooperating with the oppressors.

People I seemed to have so much in common with would catch me off guard. Like the gorgeous mother of two young children. We were both 32 and chummy, until one day I gave my opinion on how badly black people were treated. She was taken aback. "A nigger will never be welcome in my house," she blurted out. Just like that, we both knew where we stood. We had seemed so close, and we were so far apart.

Many of the people of the bayou were gentle, loving and good to me. I was treated kindly even though I thought differently and had a Yankee accent. In the pulpit, I was always honest on racial matters and reminded the parishioners that God called us to love one another. I would offer up prayers for the civil rights workers killed and ask God to help us see each other as humans.

Along the state's highways, there were large billboards that read "Martin Luther Coon." Other billboards showed Martin Luther King Jr. in alleged meetings with "Communists from Russia."

I took a drive up to Philadelphia, Mississippi, to visit a classmate, Jeffrey. It was near that city that the three civil rights workers were killed. I wanted to see for myself these places I had read so much about.

In Philadelphia, Jeffrey helped run the church in town, as well as a Native American church and school on the Choctaw Reservation. It was a glimpse of another level of oppression. It was amazing to see downtown Philadelphia, with poor blacks on one corner and poor Native Americans on another.

The area was still receiving unwanted attention because of the murders. The state had refused to prosecute the men identified as responsible for the deaths, citing a lack of evidence, but the FBI decided to bring charges. Rightly or wrongly, Philadelphia was synonymous with the Klan.

On my way back home to DeLisle, I got something in my eye. It hurt badly, so I sought out emergency help at the hospital.

"Sorry, there is no doctor here except for extreme emergencies, and we can't help you," I was told. "You could try the clinic down the road. We will call to make sure they are there."

I went down the road and came to a clinic. I went in with my Roman collar on, looking quite conspicuous. I noticed the separate colored and white waiting areas. Before I could choose, the receptionist asked, "May we help you?"

"I have something in my eye, and it hurts very much. I'm supposed to drive back to the coast now, but I can hardly see."

"Please wait, and I will be right back," she said.

Before long, she returned and said, "Please come back with me, and the doctor will see you immediately."

I walked down the hall and was ushered into an examination room. The nurse said, "Father, please lie down on this table."

I climbed up on the table and lay on my back, grateful to be there. All seemed neat and clean. The nurse came back with the doctor, and he began to examine me. It was clear I was an outsider and from the North. The nurse said to me, "Father, all of us are not bad around here. May I read you a poem?"

I was surprised. I had just come in to get help with my eye, not to lecture anyone on race relations. "Yes, I would love to hear your poem."

"The poem is not mine, but Dr. Moore's," she said, then proceeded to read it. The gist of the poem was a call for all of us not only to learn to live together, but to love one another. As she read, the doctor worked on my eye. In a minute, my pain was relieved. I remained quiet and listened to the doctor and nurse explaining to me, an outsider, how it felt to live in the town at that particular time.

"The vast majority of the people in Philadelphia are ashamed of the recent killings and the sensational publicity surrounding the incident," the doctor said.

I didn't want them to feel that I was trying to judge them in any way. Some in Mississippi might not have cared what others thought of the state. They clearly did. "I'm just passing through," I told them. "You have helped me in my pain. I will ever be grateful to you for your kindness."

"I am putting this patch over your one eye, so be careful," the doctor said. "Your depth perception will be somewhat off as you drive." We shook hands, and I said goodbye to Philadelphia.

Back in DeLisle, life was peaceful.

Down the street and around the corner from our rectory was a gas station, the only place in town to buy gas with its old pumps and RC Cola signs. I would shout greetings to Annie, the woman who owned the station, whenever I stopped at the pumps.

"Hi, Père" would always be the response. "How are you, Père?" It was the French title for priest.

When I brought her Holy Communion, Annie would stop and recite the incredibly long ancient Oath Against Modernism: "I firmly embrace and accept each and every definition that has been set forth and declared by the unerring teaching authority of the Church, especially those principal truths which are directly opposed to the errors of this day.

"And first of all, I profess that God, the origin and end of all things, can be known with certainty by the natural light of reason from the created world, that is, from the visible works of creation, as a cause from its effects, and that, therefore, his existence can also be demonstrated.

"Secondly, I accept and acknowledge…" And on and on she would go. Annie would recite this oath in her more comfortable French.

Her husband sat in a rocking chair inside the little store, among the moon pies, cokes, potato chips and snuff. He never said much and did less but was always smiling and cheerful. Annie ran the show.

Another Annie also was a big part of our lives. Each afternoon, one of the priests would say to me, "Let's go swimming at Annie's pool and eat supper at her restaurant. The other Trinitarian priests of the area will be there."

It was a pleasant outing at first, then it became a problem for me. This Annie and her husband had a wonderful restaurant in Pass Christian. She loved the Trinitarian priests and welcomed them any time of the day or night. They could swim in the couple's private pool, eat in their restaurant and have drinks served from the bar. Most of this cost the priests nothing. It was not long before I felt that too much drinking was going on. While the food and swimming were great, it struck me that we were taking advantage of this fine woman whose husband was perpetually drunk.

Some of the other priests said to me, "Keil, you're just a goddamn hypocrite."

"What's wrong with a few drinks?" some asked. "We don't have easy lives being priests in Mississippi. Why don't you want to have fun? A little swimming, eating and drinking won't hurt you."

In a sense, I felt that they were right. I did feel like a hypocrite because sometimes I met women and was attracted to them. I felt guilty and ashamed about that. On the other hand, I knew that many priests had problems with alcohol, and I knew that I was as vulnerable as anyone. I knew I needed to stay away from liquor. If I drank, I might find myself hopping into bed with some woman. Hypocrite or not, I wanted to stay focused.

I had long conversations about life, theology and race relations with the other priests. I would state my feeling and thoughts and sometimes hear, "Keil, you're just a goddamn nigger lover. You've got to get it through your thick head that you are young and you are not going to change Mississippi."

Still I wanted to try to address issues of justice, even if I didn't know how. I knew I needed to spend this first summer learning and being guided. I would have talks with Mela in the rectory. She told me about the priest at her church. He was Father McCloon, a Josephite priest living in Pass Christian. The Josephites were a religious congregation dedicated to service in the African-American community. They were mostly white but had some black clergy.

Mela said to me, "Father Keil, you got to meet Father McCloon. He don't take nothing off nobody. You'd like him. I'll tell him about you."

Soon, I went to see Father McCloon at his rectory. When he opened the door, I thought, God, he's big. He must be 6 feet 3 inches and 260 pounds.

"Hi, Keil," he said, reaching out with his big paw. His smile was friendly and his short crew cut hair revealed some gray. He had to stop talking as the train went by only 30 feet away from the house.

Then he continued, "Mela told me about you. Don't let the other priests get to you about racial issues. I have been called a nigger priest all my life. It didn't stop me from bringing Head Start to Mississippi, even though the other priests and the Bishop told me I was wrong. The KKK has attacked me, but I beat the hell out of one of the guys who jumped me."

Father McCloon knew what it felt like to be isolated. He thought I should get to know more people. "We have some wonderful black churches here," he said. "Would you like to say Mass for me one weekend when I'm gone? Usually, I have to ask the Divine Word Missionaries at Bay St. Louis to say Mass because many of the other white priests won't come to the black churches. They say they are too busy, but I know better because some have told me."

I was being educated again.

"I've got to have a drink, Keil, would you like something?" Father asked.

"Maybe water or Coke," I responded.

"Yeah, Keil, I drink too much, but it helps the pressure I'm under. I try to watch what I drink."

Father McCloon didn't watch carefully enough. He died because of the stuff a number of years later, another casualty on a seemingly endless list of alcoholic priests.

Listening to Father McCloon talk about the seminary at Bay St. Louis piqued my interest in finding out a bit more about these black priests and their religious order. I drove over to their seminary and was captivated by this lovely place near the water.

I was immediately invited to stay for supper. I was introduced to Father Joseph Francis, Father Smith, Father Olivier and maybe a dozen other priests. Father Harold Perry – I first met him in Baltimore – was to be the first black Catholic Bishop in the United States since Bishop Healy many years earlier. Father Francis was also to become a Bishop. I felt so happy that I could learn now directly from these black clergy about issues in the Church and society. It was a learning experience not to be equaled.

At supper, I sat next to a handsome, young black priest named Jim Burns. We introduced ourselves and struck up a friendship.

"What are you doing tomorrow?" he asked.

"I say Mass at the convent early, but I could get away for a few hours in the morning if you are free," I said.

We met at the seminary the next morning and went down to walk by the beautiful water on Bay St. Louis. I asked him about his job.

"I'm in charge of recruiting seminarians throughout the United States. Our order has always been concerned about the lack of black clergy in the Catholic Church. While we encourage all young men who may be interested in our order to join us, there has been a distinct lack of black priests in the Church. Our order provides a safe, challenging and loving environment for black young men wishing to study for the priesthood. Some of us have become bishops. But, as of now, we are made bishops only in foreign lands.

"The church in the United States provides a difficult environment for priests to survive and make progress. Our priests are often refused access to white churches."

My assignment to Mississippi again was more fruitful than I had ever dreamed. Here I was, learning about the state of black clergy in the Catholic Church directly from the black clergy, not from second-hand accounts from white priests who may have been biased and who may not have even known any black priests.

Though I was in a small town, priests were constantly coming and going. One day, Father Hubert asked me to go to the New Orleans airport to pick up Father Mathis, who was coming to help while Father Hubert and another priest were on vacation.

I knew Father Mathis. He was one of the professors of Canon Law in the seminary, though I had never had him for that class. He was moody and usually had a red face and nose from his clandestine drinking. As seminarians, we did not socialize with the priests, but we saw many who were like Father Mathis. They were trying to teach seminarians how to be holy and content and yet many were profoundly unhappy themselves.

At seminary once, Father Mathis told me, "Brother, you have never had me for class. But, you know, I would always give you a B for a grade, even if you aren't a scholar, because you are such a good guy." I thanked him for his words because, at the time, it was the only acceptable response a seminarian could give a priest. I was grateful because he felt I was a good person and had noticed me in the anonymous seminary setting. But I also felt insulted because it was yet another Trinitarian priest judging my intellectual capacities without knowing me. While I might not have been eloquent, I was hardly dumb. In fact, I had always been quite a good student when I put my mind to it.

At the airport, Father Mathis was easy to spot with his tall Irish good looks, his red face and clerical garb. When he started to talk, his slurred speech and the alcohol on his breath were obvious. His gait was unsteady.

"Father," he said, "I want to go to downtown New Orleans. I have a friend who owns a nice restaurant. Just drive me downtown, and we can eat there."

Obedience was so ingrained in me, having been out of the seminary for only a few weeks, that I agreed, even though he was drunk.

We were constantly taught that the priests over us reflected the will of God. The message: There's no need use your own judgment; just follow orders. It was a sick teaching, and it went to the heart of my sickness – the constant need to please.

I responded to Father Mathis, "I'll drive you to this restaurant, and, if there is something else you need, let me know."

We drove downtown, parked the car and began to look for the restaurant. We looked here and there, and it became apparent that Father Mathis wasn't sure of the location. We tried one last place that Father insisted was the right one. Standing there was a gorgeous, luscious, half-clad bunny. I was not so innocent that I did not recognize Father Mathis had led us, in our clerical suits and collars, into a Playboy Club.

"Father Mathis, let's get out of here. We're in the wrong place, and we had better head home right now."

I was feeling embarrassed and disgusted. Not that the women made me feel this way, but because it was sick, drunken behavior that had led us there. We went to the car, and I drove home to DeLisle and Our Lady of Good Hope Church.

Father's drinking persisted. Priests gathered and imbibed into the wee hours. I was judgmental and self-righteous. I was new, but had already lived with and seen so much drunkenness in the clergy.

I seethed one night as I tried to sleep through loud talk and laughter in another room. I had a 5:30 a.m. Mass to say 40 miles away, meaning that I would have to rise about 4 a.m. To my embarrassment, it was red-eyed Father Mathis who woke me up at 4:30. For some reason, my alarm didn't go off. If Father Mathis hadn't been drinking all night and remembered that I had the early Mass, I would have slept straight through my obligation.

CHAPTER 15

THE TRINITARIAN HOUSE WAS ON Rock Creek Church Road in Washington, D.C., across from the Soldiers' Home. Established as an "asylum for old and disabled veterans" in 1851, the grounds of Soldiers' Home were beautiful and well-kept, the perfect place for peaceful walks. President Lincoln would go there often for relaxation during his trying years in the White House. The serenity there contrasted greatly with the angst that often filled the Trinitarian House.

There were seven in my ordination class. The superiors assigned four of us to degree programs and the other three, including me, to general pastoral studies at Catholic University. We lived under the paternalistic watch of two priests who ordered Haig & Haig scotch by the case.

It was a sad joke, but at least as priests, and no longer seminarians, we could mostly ignore their drunken grouchiness and sanctimonious lecturing.

Now we could really experience Washington. We could explore its museums and galleries, enjoy movies and the National Symphony, spend time in the coffee houses and bookstores. We were expected to sign out, detailing where we were going and how much money we were taking, but it felt wonderful to have this limited autonomy. We even had private rooms.

I loved my classes, the studying and meeting other students. I frequented a little snack bar on campus and enjoyed sitting among lay students from all over the world and religious sisters, brothers and priests from dozens of different orders and dioceses.

As we sat drinking coffee and eating tuna salad sandwiches, conversation was lively. In the 1960s, there was plenty to talk about, be it world, national or church politics. I mainly sat and listened, but sometimes gave my account of my summer in Mississippi.

I noticed a Franciscan sister was often in the cafeteria. Across the room, I would see her leading spirited discussions and pounding her fists on the table. Her religious habit, youth and good looks made her even more intriguing.

I was sitting with a couple of friends having coffee when she passed our table one day and acknowledged my friends. They introduced us. Her name was Monica.

"You're the priest who was in Mississippi and wants to go back!" Sister Monica said to me.

I smiled and said, "Yes, that's right. How do you know that?"

"Friends told me they had met someone they liked and told me about you," Monica said. "May I join you for coffee?"

We all nodded. "Yes, by all means."

I don't remember what we were debating that day. Though I had seen an animated version of Sister Monica leading discussions, she spoke sparingly that afternoon, content with listening.

Some days later, when I was drinking coffee alone, she stopped by my table and struck up a conversation.

"I am on the General Council of the Franciscans from Philadelphia. I'm here at Catholic University because my order wants me to be an administrator and address some issues in our convents, churches, schools and hospitals," she said after we'd been talking for a while. "There are many problems. Our sisters are often hurt and abused. Many of the clergy do not understand us."

Sister Monica, who was also a member of the National Sister Formation Conference, was searching for ways to help improve the lives of nuns and to increase sisters' autonomy. I was happy to be her sounding board. Nuns dealt with many of the same problems brothers and priests encountered. Often, their situations were worse.

It seems impossible, but I would later encounter sisters who were paid only $75 a month and, in some instances, required to help pay lay teachers out of their own meager salaries.

Sister Monica liked my frankness when we spoke about these issues. She also wanted to know more about me. "Tell me about Mississippi. Why do you want to go back there? You are smart and talented. You could get a nice position here in Washington. In fact, we would hire you as the spiritual director at our Motherhouse and college."

I was flattered. "You're very kind, but I feel there are needs in other places. I don't want to be an administrator. I just want to be a pastor in poor churches and address issues of injustice.

"I've seen so much neglect there," I continued. "Often, it seems, the best priests are saved for administration and seminary work, and I feel that they should be sent into pastoral situations to put their talent to use there."

Talking to Monica then and later was very affirming for me. The seminary can beat the confidence out of you. Here was another nun assuring me I was intelligent, approachable and offered good counsel.

The work I did outside of my studies, as a priest, also helped me gain confidence. I was a chaplain at Holy Cross and Providence hospitals. It was beautiful work, and there were always profound learning opportunities. I responded to sickness, murders, rapes, mental illness and family crises.

I would report to work at 4 p.m. on Fridays and get off at 2 p.m. on Sundays. Chaplains got little sleep, if any. It was challenging work, but it reminded me of the reasons I wanted to become a priest.

The chaplains were to visit all of the patients; we also could be summoned to any room or unit if there was an emergency or patients wanted to talk. One night about 11:30 p.m., my phone rang. "Father, go to room 321. A priest is asking to see you."

Soon I was knocking on the door of 321. "Hi, are you awake?"

"Yes, come in and thanks for coming" was the reply

The room was dark except for the nightlight. "The light hurts me right now," the man said. Squinting in the dark, I could see that his face and eyes were badly swollen.

"Golly, are you all right?"

"I'm fine," he said. "I want to get out of here, but it's the best place to heal. I want to talk with someone, but I don't want you to feel sorry for me."

I sat down to listen.

"I work at St. Anthony's Church, a rough neighborhood. I love working there, but some guys were robbing the school, and I came upon them in the parking lot and one of them threw a cement block at me and caught my face."

"I am so sorry that happened," I said.

He shrugged it off. "If we want to work in the inner city, we must be ready for this. If we wish to touch areas of society where there is much pain, we will feel some of it."

Still I could see that, late at night, sitting alone in a hospital room, the work could take its toll and make a person feel very alone.

For about an hour, he talked about his life and his family and his hopes as a priest. I didn't say much more. He was teaching me such a beautiful lesson about sacrifice. We prayed and said goodnight at about 1 a.m.

Another night at the hospital, the phone rang at 2 a.m. I was so tired when I reached to pick it up. "Father, come down to the emergency room. There's a lady here with chest pains. She wants to see you."

I rolled out of bed with my clothes on. I found it easier to sleep on top of the bed, fully dressed and ready to go. The nurse greeted me when I came to the emergency room and took me behind a maze of curtains separating the patients. "Mrs. Kruger, this is Father Keil," the nurse said. "He will help you."

Mrs. Kruger did not look very old, maybe 55. She was not on the examination table but was sitting in a wheelchair in a hospital gown. She seemed fine, but I was about to find out that looks can be deceptive.

"Hi, Father, I am very glad to see you. I came for chest pains, but now I'm feeling fine. They told me they are keeping me for a few days for observation. I wanted to see a priest right away, so I'm happy you came."

"I'm happy to be here and glad you called. How can I help you?"

"I was frightened so I asked to see a priest," she said. "But it is so late in the night, and I feel I'm just bothering you."

I assured her she was not.

"I would like to make a confession, if I may. Is there any way I may receive communion in the morning?"

"I brought communion with me," I responded. "Why don't you begin your confession? If we keep our voices low, no one can hear. Take your time, and we can do all the sacraments. We can even anoint you."

Mrs. Kruger began. "Bless me, Father, for I have sinned…"

After talking with her for about an hour, I went back to bed a little after 3:30 a.m. About 5:30 a.m., the phone rang again. It was the nurse. "Father, come to the emergency room. Mrs. Kruger died, and her children are here."

I was stunned. I walked into a private room to see the family. I could see they were shocked and saddened, but someone said kindly, "Thank you for seeing our mother during the night. We never expected this."

We talked for a while about life and death and life's mysteries. I went back to my room glad that I had been called to see Mrs. Kruger and glad that I hadn't been dismissive.

I spent many weekends either at the hospitals, but still had a full schedule at Catholic University. During my year of classes there, I kept my eyes and ears open for new learning experiences. I had heard that the scripture courses taught by Father Quinlan were very good. I decided take advantage of a policy that allowed students who were not enrolled in a class to sit in and listen.

Father Quinlan was tall, bald and had an Irish accent. He had taught Dogmatic Theology for 18 years in a large Irish seminary before coming to Catholic University.

He prided himself on teaching his classes with "intellectual honesty."

"The Pope has written against birth control, and the bishops of America strictly adhere to the Pope's words," he said. But, he added, he disagreed with the Church's teaching that certain birth control should not be used, and he felt compelled to speak out.

Father Quinlan took a stand against the Church's teachings. He became a role model for many because he examined his own conscience and stood up for what he believed was right, despite the Church's pronouncements. He was dismissed from the university because of it, but provided a powerful example.

Everyone at Catholic University knew Father Gilbert Hartke. He often came to class in his long white Dominican habit. If he said, "Gregory and I are having lunch today," or "Ed and I are having supper," or "Loretta called me," he meant actor Gregory Peck, comedian Ed McMahon and actress Loretta Young.

Father Hartke was chairman of the Speech and Drama Department. He built the department from almost nothing, and it became a place that brought great acclaim and revenue to the university.

I signed up for Advanced Public Speaking because I felt I was weak in that area and thought it would be great to take lessons from the master. Our first class was spent introducing ourselves.

The first student got up, "I'm Joe Jones, the anchor on the 6 o'clock news." A gorgeous young sister got up saying, "Hi, I'm Sister Joan. I am in my last year of my doctoral studies in communication."

I thought to myself, how the hell did I get accepted into this class?

We were required to give a speech during every class. Father Hartke and all the students were upbeat and encouraging, unlike in seminary, where everyone was hypercritical.

I gave a talk one afternoon and, after I finished, Father Hartke stopped me before I could take my seat. "Stay up front for a moment, Father Keil."

I briefly thought he was going to chew me out.

"Father, I want you to listen to me. I think you sometimes spend time trying to give speeches like the others here in class. I have noticed you, and you have a special way all your own. It's just a gift that you have. Don't change it. You also have great eye contact, and you have a wonderful voice. As public speakers, we all strive to be sincere. It's not always easy, but you have this quality."

I began to feel like I was walking on air. Here was this priest, an expert in speech and drama, a speaking coach to presidents and movie stars, telling me to remain true to myself. He was telling me that I had communication gifts. Through the years, I always kept that affirmation in my heart whenever I would speak in the pulpit.

In Dr. Robert McAllister's psychology class, it sometimes felt as though he was looking into my soul and reading my mind. This was the first psychiatrist I had ever met.

Dr. McAllister often read us papers he had presented at different conventions or seminars. He brought some of his patients to class. I thought it was brilliant that he would actually invite psychiatric patients to talk to us. One day, a lovely young woman told us the story of her struggles as a lesbian.

Given that we were at a Catholic university, one of the students asked her how she handled the Church. She began to cry. I felt uncomfortable – I was the only clergy in class and had my clerical collar on. She finally regained composure.

"I was brought up Catholic and always went to church," she said. "As I got older, I found out that I liked women, and I began to go to gay bars near Dupont Circle. After I went, I would often go to confession. The priests always told me to stay away from those bars. Some months ago, I went to confession, and the priest made me promise not to go to the bars anymore. He said if I didn't, he would not give me absolution for my sins.

"I couldn't promise, and he dismissed me. I left the confessional and church crying and walked several blocks to a gay bar. I was talking and drinking for a long while. As I got up to go to the restroom, I noticed this man. Yes, it was the very priest who had refused me absolution, sitting at the bar with a man. I just ran home all torn apart."

By this time, I wanted to crawl under a desk and hide. I promised myself that I would never refuse absolution to anyone, and I would always be accepting of gays. Dr. McAllister drove home the point to us. "All of you who chose your sexual preference," he said, "please raise your hands." No one raised his or her hand.

All around me, priests, nuns and lay people at the university seemed to be challenging the status quo, questioning the way gay people were treated, protesting the Church's birth control teaching, marching for civil rights and making a stand against the war in Vietnam. As one Church historian has said, people started adding other adjectives in front of the word Catholic: traditional Catholic or social justice Catholic or liberal or conservative.

Later, I took a marriage counseling class that Dr. McAllister taught. In it, there was a handsome young priest who often asked questions in class, and over the course of time he revealed he had been ordained five years before.

On our way to class one day, he introduced himself. "I'm James Kavanaugh. I am from Michigan."

I introduced myself, and we continued to talk for several minutes. After that, we would greet each other warmly in class. Not too many years later, publishing under a pseudonym, he rose to fame after writing a Saturday Evening Post article, "I Am a Priest, and I Want to Marry." He later wrote the book "A Modern Priest Looks at His Outdated Church" under his own name. It was No. 1 on The New York Times' best-seller list.

Many in the church lambasted Kavanaugh as lustful, disrespectful and ignorant. I thought his writings showed courage and honesty.

The cafeteria of the National Shrine of the Immaculate Conception was another popular place for students and visitors to eat or talk over coffee. One day, an elderly black man standing in front of me in line dropped his tray of food. I began helping him pick up some of the pieces, and soon there was a sister at our side, also helping. She introduced herself. "I am Sister Michael Gabriel. This is my father, George Dubrey."

"I am glad to help," I said, introducing myself. "Do you go to Catholic University?"

"No, I went some years ago. I am visiting my father here in Washington. I live in Rice Lake, Wisconsin."

I smiled and told her I was from Wisconsin and had relatives who lived close to Rice Lake. My parents were 200 miles aways in Villard, Minnesota, population 280. They had moved there for retirement. Villard didn't have many conveniences. There may have been a grocery store and pharmacy in the town, along with several businesses catering to the needs of the area farmers.

With my parents being elderly, I usually spent most of my vacation time with them. I had been away from them for so long it seemed, for two years while overseas in the Army and for ten years of seminary life.

"What do you do up there?" I asked.

"Father, I am the Mother Superior of the Rice Lake Franciscans."

I wondered how this beautiful, young black sister from Washington, D.C., had become the Mother Superior of an order in northern Wisconsin. She was one of very few African Americans in the whole of north Wisconsin. We continued to talk for a while and exchanged addresses. I told her I'd be coming up to see family and asked if I could visit while I'm there.

"Father, I would love to see you and to show you our place," she responded. "It is on a lovely island on Rice Lake."

We became beloved friends over the years. One day, when I was in Alabama, I received a call from her.

"Father, the past years I have shared many aspects of my life and different aspects of our religious order with you. Having prayed and talked with the Bishop, I feel that it is best that our order merge with another order. The other order is larger than we are, and it would benefit us immensely," she said.

"I am volunteering to give up my position as Mother Superior and am taking a job as a nurse on the night shift at the new order's hospital in Aurora, Illinois."

I was surprised by the news and astonished at Sister Michael Gabriel's maturity and grace. Her attitude was so refreshing, so different from others in the Church who were in positions of authority and engaged in power struggles. She was willing to give up her position when it was evident that it was better for all concerned.

My first year of ordination and Catholic University gave me a chance to meet beautiful, genuine people who would become powerful role models. They showed me the kind, compassionate side of the Church that I so missed. Under their loving tutelage, I started to regain a sense of self-worth. It also became clear to me that not only was it OK to challenge the status quo, it was my responsibility. I felt refreshed and encouraged as I headed back to Mississippi.

CHAPTER 16

IT WAS A SATURDAY MORNING in sleepy Kiln, Mississippi, the end of a busy week.

My time had been stretched between driving dusty miles visiting parishioners in their homes, helping Sister Claire and our four new teachers in the parish school and meeting with people for counseling sessions. Now the phone was ringing again. I picked up, and Sister Marie James was on the other end.

"Father," she said breathlessly, "will you go up to Rocky Hill with me to see Mrs. Ladner? She just called and is very upset. She says Robert has been drinking all night, and he is yelling and threatening her and the children.

"He will listen to you," she was saying. "I am afraid to go up there alone because I know that he can be ugly."

I knew Robert and his family. He was a large man with dark hair and eyes. Mabel, his wife, was beautiful, as were their five children. They were poor, but the children were intelligent and doing well in our school.

"Sister," I said, "I will go with you, but I don't think I will be of much help. If the guy is drunk, the police will do better than we can."

"Please, Father, come with me. I think we can help. And Robert likes you."

I had been in Kiln only a short time, but the people of the parish had adopted me. The letter assigning me there came in 1966: "After prayer and guidance of the Holy Spirit, and with consultation with the General Council, I am asking you to report to Annunciation Parish in Kiln, Mississippi."

Since I had spent the previous summer in DeLisle, Mississippi, I was already familiar with the area. I knew Kiln had a poor, all-white church, and that priests there served five smaller rural parishes. While I had once again hoped I would be assigned to a black parish, and could be more involved in the fight for racial equality, I was content with the assignment.

The pastor of the church was Father Canisius. I had met him briefly the previous summer in Philadelphia, Mississippi, the town where three civil rights workers had been killed. He was a brave and dedicated priest who had tried to help the people there weather the terrible times. He, like my friend Jeffrey, also served the Choctaw Indians, who had a reservation right outside of town.

I grew to love the people of Kiln and learned much from them. Southern Mississippi was unlike any other place I knew. A number of folks in the area made their living by selling moonshine. Sometimes, parents would come to the school and hurriedly demand that their children be excused for the day so they could rush home and help break up the moonshine stills before the Feds arrived. In Kiln, there was profound poverty right alongside extreme wealth.

On my first night there, a Friday, I drove to the Annunciation School playground, a local gathering place. Getting out of the car, I headed toward a group of men standing around a barbecue grill. It smelled good. Some of the men were drinking beer. Father Canisius was standing next to the men, laughing and talking. He spotted me and said, "Hey everyone, here is our new priest."

I was usually shy in larger groups, but I greeted them warmly.

"Hi, Father. Hope you like Kiln," one of them said.

"All priests like Kiln," someone else said. "We're different around here."

A large man picked up some meat on the grill and said, "Here, Father, have something to eat."

I reached out to take the plate of meat, and he grinned, "It's goat meat, Father, and you ain't supposed to eat meat on Friday."

He laughed and laughed, and the other guys began to laugh, too, at the thought of a priest coming so close to eating meat on a Friday. I laughed, as well. But, at the same time, I was glad that he stopped me. I didn't know if I would like goat meat.

As I met the people, I noticed the some of the same names as in DeLisle: Cuevas, Dubuisson, Duhon and Ladner. Many of them were related to one another, descended from Cajun and Spanish settlers. For generations, they had been a part of the bayou country of southern Mississippi and Louisiana with its crawfish, shrimp, oysters, fishing of all sorts, alligators and large oaks with draping Spanish moss. It was a land of small farms, fresh vegetables, and strong, thick chicory coffee.

I was a young white priest, a Yankee with social change on my mind. My agenda revolved around issues of liberation. But I realized that I first needed to get to know the people and live life with them, not to jam sociological pablum down their throats. Each day, I would drive or walk down red clay roads and talk to residents. I learned about their passions, their gifts, their limitations, their struggles.

Robert Ladner's struggle was the bottle. After Sister Marie James' call, I drove to the convent, where she was waiting outside. Sister quickly got into the car, her dark hair curly and wet. She was very pretty and seemed so young and energetic, so dedicated. Despite the early hour and our reason for going to Rocky Hill, she was upbeat and smiling.

It was a little bit of a drive, but finally we pulled off the muddy clay road into the Ladners' driveway. The whole family was on the porch. The children were crying, and wife and husband were standing there, looking somber.

I got out of the car and casually said, "Hey, Bob. Hey, Mabel." I went up to them and hugged them. I then went to the children and hugged them.

I took a deep breath, then turned to the children. "Would you help me and your parents and go inside while we talk out here? I love you all, and we will just be talking."

Sister led them into the house. When she came out, I suggested that she and Mabel talk, then I turned to the hulking man in front of me. "Robert, why don't you and I walk out back, by your garden?"

"OK, Father. If you think it's best."

This drunken lion had turned into a pussycat when Sister and I drove into their yard. There was no defensiveness or drunken bravado. His speech was broken and a little slurred, but coherent. We went out the back door to the wooden porch, down the rickety steps to their large backyard. The garden had an abundance of tomatoes, corn, lettuce, okra, beans and lovely flowers.

Robert said, "Father, let me get you some 'maters and pole beans before you go. We got so much. I'm telling you, Mabel cooked us a lot last night."

"Thanks, Robert. I'd be glad to take some back. I appreciate your kindness. Sister tells me that you and Mabel were having an argument, and that you were very mad."

"Aw, Father, I'm so sorry. I work my ass off all week. I got two jobs, one in Pascagoula at the shipyard and then I repair cars here at the house. See that Chevy over there next to the tree? I got to get on that today. The kids need something all the damn time, and Mabel worries about money. I ain't made out of money. I had a few beers. It helps me relax. But then

I get pissed off 'cause they need so much, and I ain't got it. I feel like shit, and I yell. You know I won't hurt them."

"Robert, I believe you if you say you won't hit them," I told him. "On the other hand, why don't you say to them what you just said me instead of yelling at them?"

Robert looked down with shame and mumbled, "Yeah, I guess so. I want to do right, but I just get mad and forget. And I don't know all the stuff you know. I never went to school much."

I continued, "Robert, you are smart, and your kids are smart. They do good in school. Do they get all that from Mabel or is some of it from you?"

He smiled and looked up. "Do you think I'm smart? I never thought of that, and no one ever said it."

"You are plenty smart, and so is Mabel," I said. "We all have to learn each day. Maybe they need to learn that money doesn't grow on trees. Isn't it fair that you may have something to learn also, about not yelling, or is it only the wife and children who have to learn? You say that you don't hit them, but your talk can hurt them almost as much. Your threats to Mabel scare the children to death.

"You may not believe it, but you are so nice when you aren't drinking that they just don't know what to do when you drink and get ugly. Tell them you are afraid that you don't do enough for them. Tell them that they can't have everything they want. Tell them that their asking for stuff all the time makes you angry and frustrated."

I could see that he was feeling contrite.

"Robert, I would be glad meet with all of you tomorrow afternoon. We can change some things, make them better. Give me a chance. Give yourself a chance, your family a chance.

"I'm talking too darn much, but I love you and your family. You all don't deserve to be unhappy when all of you are so good-hearted."

Robert was crying. I was crying. We hugged one another, dried our eyes and began walking to the house.

"Let's go talk with Mabel," Robert said.

CHAPTER 17

FATHER JOHN WAS GOOD-HEARTED, BUT he was a fool, to hear our novice master, Father Jacob, tell it.

Such pronouncements from him during our year of novitiate training were not out of character. Red-nosed Father Jacob often would cast judgment, putting down others as he casually sipped martinis. We were all trained to laugh and smile at his comments, or risk ending up on his "bad" list. He had certain young men whom the rest of us jokingly referred to as his pets. They were spared his smug scrutiny. Most others, including Father John, was not.

In 1950, Father John bought a run-down, abandoned public school for $1 from the Hancock County Board of Commissioners. I guess buying an old school in Mississippi may have seemed foolish. But later, during my time as a priest in Kiln, I discovered it was a wise and visionary move.

Several of the priests who succeeded Father John as pastor in the small town put money and energy into renovating the building. It became a much-needed facility for the rural children of Hancock County and cost just a fraction of what the Trinitarians might have spent.

The principal of the school was a Trinitarian sister, Claire Frances. There were only four teachers for all eight grades. They were new each year, young Catholic women who had finished college back east or maybe in the Midwest, then volunteered through the Catholic Church Extension Society. They worked for free, stayed on a year and taught two grades.

Annunciation School was better than the local public schools, but teaching there would still try the patience of a saint. The children were products of a local culture in which education was not high on the list of essentials.

By default, the students who got into trouble ended up being referred to me. Father Canisius, the pastor, had suffered a heart attack and was sidelined while he recovered. Sister Claire was sickly and often in the hospital.

Each night, around suppertime, I met with the teachers. It seemed like I was always begging one of them not to throw in the towel, not to head straight to the closest airport and fly home that night. We had many close calls.

"I can't take it! I can't take it! I have tried my best, and I am failing," they would say. "The children don't want to learn. The parents don't care."

Bettina, the lovely dark-haired ballerina from Connecticut, would break down, cry, then smile and declare her intent to stay. Carol, the millionaire's daughter from Chicago, would get teary-eyed, then toughen up, never willing to use her money to dodge responsibilities. Mary from Philadelphia sometimes thought she would rather go back to Philly and play with men. Then she would smile and say, "Ok, I'll stay if you continue to help us every day."

Of course, I planned to help every day. I was acting pastor, assistant pastor, sometime principal and eighth-grade teacher, all in my first year of pastoral work. I knew little about teaching, but did my best. I would visit each grade to greet students. I would praise them, laugh with them and encourage them to behave. I would tell them that we expected good grades and hard work.

A few older boys did try to take advantage of the upheaval that followed Father Canisius' absence and refused to obey the teachers. Even though the parents and principal encouraged me to, I never hit a child. I remembered my lesson from Fides House. I usually made the boys run around the gym until they were so tired that they promised to behave. After several trips to the gym, coupled with my visits with students in the mornings, things settled down.

The people of Kiln were dear to me, and I was also working with the most wonderful pastor in the world in Father Canisius. I learned from him how to counsel young married couples, how to deal with parishioners and how to state my views about racial equality and genuinely listen to those with different views, those who were less genteel than Jack Miller, my friend from Phenix City. I learned how to sit with discomfort. I learned to appreciate the people, one person at a time, not putting anyone in a group with a label attached.

I talked, ate, cried and laughed with the families. The richer folks from Mississippi and Louisiana looked down on these rural people, many of whom did not have electricity until after WWII. But the people of Kiln were loving and full of life. They survived their poverty by leaning on each other. Cookouts were common, along with turkey shoots to raise money for neighbors who had suffered tragedies.

True, many of the poor people of the area manufactured moonshine to make money. But I didn't protest that too much. I detest the oceans of pain and suffering alcohol brings. But, in my view, these country people were just growing corn and grain and "harvesting" it in a different manner than making feed or popcorn.

I was with the people of Kiln for just more than a year, but some memories are permanently ingrained. I will never forget the touching Christmas program the children gave. An 11-year-old boy beautifully sang "Bring a Torch, Jeanette, Isabella." There has not been a time since 1966 that I am not reminded of Kiln when I hear that song.

I think back fondly of the two pretty, blonde sisters, Cathy and Beth Favre, who lived close to the rectory and would often stop by to talk to me if I had time. Their father and mother were beloved, as their dad helped lead efforts to promote dialogue between the black and white communities. The girls made me a stuffed Humpty Dumpty that I have it to this day.

I was constantly visiting homes and meeting new, precious people. I remember giving marriage instructions to a beautiful couple, marrying them on a Saturday, only to have the groom killed in an auto accident as they drove to the reception. It was a grim lesson for all of us. Life is so tenuous and unpredictable. Love is all that survives.

While I was in Kiln, I met a Dominican sister teaching in a public school. Years before, as a college student, she had been chosen Mardi Gras queen by a prestigious New Orleans krewe. She taught me many things about southern culture. She was also an exceptional scholar of scripture. I had just finished 11 years of theology and philosophy studies, but felt she knew more than many of my professors.

I enjoyed her company immensely. Once, when we attended the same conference, we took a walk alone along a Gulf Coast shore and talked. Later, I felt guilty about it. On the one hand, it all seemed so natural. But I couldn't help feeling that I was doing something wrong by simply enjoying her company.

I struggled with these types of feelings during all of my years as a seminarian and priest. I was trained that celibacy was an obligation, a struggle and a sacrifice. I thought the pain of loneliness was a natural consequence, the price of being a priest. The Dominican sister ended up going to South America. Last I heard, she married a priest down there and was happy. I do not know where she went after that.

In April 1967, Father Canisius pulled me aside and told me that he had recommended me to the Superior General to become head of Holy Trinity, the founding place of the Trinitarians. This was the last thing I expected him to say. I was even more surprised when the Trinitarians chose me.

CHAPTER 18

PHENIX CITY HAD ITS BARS, pawn shops and other trappings to attract soldiers from nearby Fort Benning, Georgia. But for the most part, Russell County, Alabama, was as rural as it could possibly be in 1967. The sun rose and set over quiet fields and desolate back roads, with only the occasional car on Highway 165. At night, the moon gazed down on land that was hushed and still except for the crickets and whip-poor-wills.

I never ceased to be amazed when, driving down lonely red clay roads, I stumbled onto a family living and surviving a couple of miles into the woods in a sharecropper cabin. These people knew a hard and simple way of life. Usually, water came from a nearby creek. Wood was gathered and chopped for cooking and heating. Laundry was dropped in boiling water in large black kettles. Inside the cabin, old newspapers sometimes lined the walls as insulation. In addition to family pictures, there might be a picture of President

John F. Kennedy. Soon, Martin Luther King Jr.'s picture would be added and Bobby Kennedy's shortly after.

Never for a day, during my years of study, had I not thought about returning to Russell County to live and work. Coming back to Holy Trinity was a blessing, or it might have been a curse. Then and now, I look at it as the will of God. I was named pastor of a black church smack in the middle of George Wallace country. The governor who had declared, "Segregation now, segregation tomorrow, segregation forever," was born just 60 miles down the road. No time in my life, and no place I've been, is as hard to describe as rural Alabama from 1967 to 1975.

The Trinitarians honored me by making me pastor and superior of Holy Trinity, the founding place of the religious order. I was surprised, but felt ready to be pastor of the mission and approached the opportunity with confidence.

I was not ready to be the religious superior, the person charged with making sure that the customs and practices of the religious order are kept and that assignments and duties are carried out. I had not sought out that kind of power.

I lived in an old Army barracks. I knew it well, having slept there as a college seminarian some years back. I bunked in the huge building by myself. The wooden, two-story barracks was a cast off from Fort Benning, World War I vintage. The seminary had moved from Alabama in the early 1960s, leaving the rooms vacant and lonely. The order had spent about $8 million building new seminaries in Virginia and Maryland, only to find that the seminarian population was dwindling. The 1960s had brought much change to the Church, and a drop in those who wanted to become priests was one.

I had studied for and passed countless examinations on my way to the priesthood. I had educated myself about the issues affecting the black community. Now, here I was, on my own. I might not be able to change the world, I told myself, but I could help change this place. Holy Trinity was so far out in the country, few people in the world gave a darn. Sunday mornings, I could preach what I wanted. I could join any civil rights organization I wanted.

Standing on the front steps of St. Joseph's Chapel on my first Sunday in my new position, I wondered if anyone would be there to hear what I had to say.

The turnout was only eight people for Mass. But I was not discouraged. I was fully aware that the Catholic Church and the Trinitarian order had not been overly successful at attracting parishioners. Yes, some people knew the Trinitarians, but mostly because they did work for us or lived nearby.

Still I was confident that we could have a thriving community that worked together to improve conditions. It would start with Thelma, Marie Thornton, Leila Mae Lockhart, her brother Paul Anthony Lockhart, Ernest Williams and Johnny Johnson, I thought. They were black. It would start with Catherine McClendon, and Sarah and Buck Davis. They were white. They were not all Catholic and converting them was not my goal.

After Mass, I greeted each person with a hug, a laugh, some happy tears and a few words as they left the church. That's my style. Even when church attendance built up so much that it was impossible to hug each person, I would still try to make sure each person felt welcomed.

Thelma came out, and we hugged. "Oh, Father Emil, everyone is so happy that you're going to be the priest at Holy Trinity. I'm so happy. Paul Anthony can't believe it. You're so very young to be the pastor and head of Holy Trinity."

"Thanks, Thelma. I am thrilled to be here. It's hard to believe. You know how I love the people of Holy Trinity. I can't wait to talk to Paul Anthony and Leila and Ernest again and the others. Remember our trip to Panama City?" I said, thinking back to 11 years ago when I was in seminary. Thelma was still the consummate, articulate leader that she was back then, always putting everyone at ease.

Thelma smiled and, pointing to small child, said, "Father, that's my daughter, Debra. Debra, this is Father Emil. He is our friend."

"Debra, it is so nice to see you. Your pink dress is so pretty! You're a big girl," I said. She would later become the first black homecoming queen in Phenix City.

Debra smiled. "Yes, Father," she said.

I turned to Thelma, "Where is your husband? I want to meet him."

"Curtiss is down at his family's church. We go to different churches," she said. "I want you to meet him when you stop by our house. Can you come this week?"

"Yes, I would love to meet him. Where does he work, and when will he be home?"

"Curtiss works for the railroad. He has a nice job there but works nights, so he's home during the day," she said.

I told her I would call to check when they were both free. In the meantime, "I need to talk to you about what you and others think is best for Holy Trinity," I said.

I could hardly believe I was there. I was 34. Just two years earlier, I still had to ask permission from a superior to buy toothpaste. Those in charge would oversee every minute detail in a seminarian's life, making sure lights were off at a certain time. The superior would assign us our weekly work duties, and we would fetch his cigarette when he wanted one. We were like middle school students, but with no girls to flirt with. We were allowed no phone calls, even to our parents. No TV. No magazines. No newspapers. We studied, prayed, worked and lived as adolescents. Other than to run errands, the superior allowed us to go to town twice a year, the day after Christmas and the day after Easter.

Now, the six or so priests living at Holy Trinity reported to me. It was a strange feeling. The former treasurer general was here, as was Father Aspew, who was mentally ill. There was a recovering alcoholic, and another priest whose elderly mother also lived on the premises. There were also a handful of religious brothers who looked after the upkeep of the place. I wondered how I would balance all of the responsibilities facing me: the parishioners, the school, the church, the religious order, the sisters. Working to meet the needs of the local people would enliven and nourish me. Meeting the needs of the religious community would challenge me greatly.

I called Thelma later that week. "May I see you tomorrow after school to talk over how I could start here at Holy Trinity?" I asked. "There is so much to do and, while I have many ideas, I would like to see how you feel about them and listen to your ideas."

Thelma had been a teacher for a while. "Yes, Father, I could stay. We have a teachers meeting after school anyway, and I could see you after that," she answered.

The next day around 4, I was cleaning out an old office building near the school when Thelma arrive. The campus of Holy Trinity was very large, and the Superior's office was quite a distance away.

"What are you doing, Father?" Thelma asked, laughing at how messy I looked. "You're all dirty, and it's so hot in here."

"I'm going to make my office here, near the school, so people can see me easier. The sisters, the teachers, the parents, the children can all come to see me if they want. I know that people don't always feel comfortable going to the house where the priests and brothers live to ask for help or just to talk. There are the cloister rules, and people just can't walk into the buildings over there. Here, people can just knock on my door."

"That'll be great. I know someone who sews and can make curtains," Thelma said. "Or we can buy some."

"Could you buy some you think will go well in here and I will repay you? You have a good eye for that." I told her I also planned to install a small air conditioner, move in a used desk I had seen in another building, some chairs and some bookshelves.

"Wait until everyone sees this, Father! They will be happy to know that they can come to see you. The people really do feel funny going over to the priests' and brothers' building. Now they can just come over here," Thelma said.

We talked more, about the needs of the school and the community. I was happy to have Thelma's feedback. She knew the area well and was committed to making things better. I admired her for that.

"Thelma, do you know of someone who could teach preschool? You handle kindergarten so well, and Sister Alice wants to begin preschool, following the Montessori Method."

Thelma wasn't acquainted with Montessori, but she knew of a nice, young woman right out of high school who could teach preschool. "She doesn't have any college. But neither do I, and I have been teaching for four years."

"Why don't you ask her to call me? If it works out, I could help her go to school. Have you thought of going back to college? If you would, it would help the school and you, and we could help with the money."

"Oh, Father, I'm afraid of going to college," Thelma said. "The money isn't the problem. My husband would help me, and I make a small salary here at the school."

I told her she had nothing to fear; she would do well in college. And I told her, as far as I was concerned, it as part of my job to encourage education. "I'm supposed to help others do their jobs and attain their wishes in life. I appreciate you so much for your help. You help so many people – the sisters, the children, the parents. Everybody."

Thelma did end up putting her fears aside. She went to college at night at Alabama State in Montgomery. She received her bachelor and master's degree, but she paid for it herself.

During my years at Holy Trinity and elsewhere, I encountered a number of young adults who wanted to go to college but simply didn't have the means. Through my own family, I had seen the importance of a good education. My father had struggled because he was forced to leave school so early. Black parents knew that education, especially college, even possible, was even more essential for their children.

Whenever I could, I helped. Sometimes this meant offering words of encouragement, or helping a person identify the right college. Sometimes it meant helping a person get enrolled and making some initial payments. I have driven students to their campuses and put them on a buses or trains. When possible, I introduced them to people who could support them emotionally or financially.

I came across Theresa Ford in the late '60s when she was a small child. I knew her family. As she was walking to the cafeteria one day, I stopped her to say hello.

All of a sudden, she started to cry. Bending over, I asked her why she was upset. She replied that she was afraid that I was going to ask her to leave the school because she had made mistakes on her homework.

I knew Theresa was an eager learner. I gently took her hand and assured her that she was one of our best students. The sisters and other teachers were proud of her, I told her, and we all loved her. "You definitely will not have to leave the school," I said.

Theresa immediately cheered up and went off smiling to her classroom. Years later, she would say that the words I spoke to her instilled in her a security and confidence she'd never had before. She felt from me a love and approval that her own father didn't provide.

Her father struggled with substance abuse. Too many times, the shy, insecure child had seen her father in his most vulnerable state. According to a story her relatives told, even the day she was born, he had come up to the hospital three sheets to the wind. He had been hoping for a baby boy, but instead discovered he had a girl. Angry, he left the hospital.

Ever since, it seemed, the child had been trying to win his love and approval.

Theresa continued to thrive as a student and went off to Catholic school in Columbus, Georgia. I didn't see much of her after that. Then, one day, after she finished high school, I received a call from her. She explained that she didn't have the money to go to college; she planned to work to save. I didn't like her plan. So often, when a person delays his or her education, life takes over. Before you know it, school falls by the wayside. She asked if I knew anywhere she could turn for help. I told her that I would call her back.

I thought of Tuskegee, Alabama State and other possibilities. Then it came to me –Xavier University in New Orleans. It was a good school founded by Mother Katharine Drexel and staffed by the Sisters of the Blessed Sacrament. I did not know Norman Francis, the president of Xavier University, but I had met his brother, Bishop Joseph Francis, a priest with the Society of the Divine Word Missionaries.

I called Xavier University and asked for the president's office, mentioning that I was a priest. Soon, Dr. Francis was on the line. We talked for a while, with him asking me pertinent questions about my work and position in my religious order. I told him that I had known his brother when I worked in Mississippi. I told him about Theresa and her family. Then Dr. Francis did an extraordinary thing: He asked me to put

Theresa on a bus. He told me that she would not have to worry about money. I was ecstatic that he had so quickly opened his heart, and Xavier, to Theresa. He told me that he and his wife would pick up Theresa at the station.

I called Theresa and told her and her mother the news. It was almost too good to be true. We all laughed and cried. Theresa went to Xavier, excelled and was voted Miss Xavier University in her senior year. After graduation, she went on to the University of Georgia and entered law school. She quickly passed the Bar and became an attorney. She met and married a loving, adept businessman in Walter Gilstrap. To this day, we keep in touch.

Theresa is a wonderful example of what an extraordinary success a person can become if given just a little help. Finding that help for her, I felt, was one of the reasons God had called me to the priesthood. Education is essential for creating a better future. To be a good priest, I knew I needed to do more than say Mass, visit the sick and help feed the hungry. I needed to do what I could to create a better future.

CHAPTER 19

I CAN STILL HEAR THE children's voices on that cold Alabama night. Some had walked several miles to our chapel for midnight Mass. Others had trudged unlighted back roads for dreadful distances just to get to the road where the mission bus stopped.

It was my first Christmas as pastor at Holy Trinity. I knew God was with me. Everything the Bible said about love and hope, poverty and the simple pleasures seemed to apply. If it wasn't donated to our church or school, it seemed, we did not have it. Some of our parishioners still walked a quarter of a mile for water, burned firewood for heat and cooking, and gave bales of cotton to rent their cabins from the land owners.

That night particular night, the church looked beautiful with the poinsettias, the Christmas tree and the manger. A lovely scent of cedar and pine boughs filled the air. The coal furnace warmed the chapel, and steam radiators hissed as I walked up the center aisle to begin Mass.

Everything around me reminded me of how lucky I was, how much I had grown since I left Racine more than a dozen years earlier. Before the start of Mass, I had walked to the church, alongside the cemetery where members of the Trinitarian order are buried, staring up at the bright stars and wondering how I had gotten to this holy place, how I had been chosen to be pastor here when there were so many other older priests who were more worthy.

I found myself looking over into the cemetery, where each gravesite had a small granite marker noting the occupant's date of birth and death. Where these men lay was hallowed ground, the founding home of the Trinitarians. Some had served with our order's founder. They came to Alabama to dedicate themselves to serving the poor of the South.

I remember thinking long and hard that night about what kind of pastor I wanted to be. I told myself my focus always would be on poor people and their needs. I would be encouraging to the people who sought out my guidance. I also would push them to listen to their own voices and to set their own goals.

I knew it was a special time at a special place with special people. I developed many close one-on-one relationships in

Russell County, not just in the church, but in some unexpected places.

Miss Bea was large and plain looking, with graying brown hair. I had first met her when I was a seminarian and would go to the large office supply store where she worked in downtown Columbus. Our dealings were superficial, but I often wondered how this country girl from Cottonton, Alabama, rose to being the secretary and general manager of that business. A single white woman, she was held in high esteem by many in the city.

When I came back to Holy Trinity 12 years later, no longer a priest-in-training, but a priest committed to educating some of the poorest black children from the town she grew up in, I wondered what she would think. We had always been cordial before. But here I was, doing something many white people in the town thought amounted to treason. It did not take me long to find out where Miss Bea stood.

She welcomed me at the store and often gave the school extra office supplies, which she paid for herself. Time after time, she would give us a break on a price. The school was growing and seemed always in dire need of something.

She and I began to talk about race relations in the area. She knew all of Holy Trinity's white neighbors and was deeply tied to the Cottonton area. She would tell me how frustrated she was, witnessing the injustices black people endured, but not knowing what to do. She said she was happy for the opportunity to assist our school and to help as much as she could.

Bea wanted to share and extend herself in matters of racial relations, but didn't know how. It once again showed me how wrong it would be to make rash judgments about all of the town's white people. She taught me about innate goodness. She told me stories of her own poverty, living hand to mouth until the 1940s when she landed a good job. Back then, she would even chew on clay for nourishment.

Miss Bea was a person of great faith who taught Sunday School for more than 60 years. She knew the wealthy people of Columbus and the poor, some of whom she cared for after hours on her own time. I will always remember her for her generosity, her sharing, her teaching, her intelligence, her keen sense of justice.

When the store was sold to a different owner, she would sometimes share with me her struggles with the new proprietor and the new policies. I was flattered by her trust, as I was much younger and from a different background and religion.

Miss Bea and I were friends for years. I ended up speaking at her funeral. She was a generous woman who grew up among prejudice but made her own decisions about how she would view people.

CHAPTER 20

My alarm buzzed on weekday mornings at 5:30 a.m. I would kneel on the wooden floor and pray for a few minutes, then walk down the hall to a bathroom equipped with multiple sinks, showers and toilets. It had once served numerous college students but now was my personal bathroom. The walls were painted a light green, and the floor was covered in a cheap brown tile except for those places where it was missing, leaving the hardened adhesive. The showers were lined with tin, rusting in some places with all the pipes exposed. Everything smelled musty and old.

After a shower, I shaved and brushed my teeth, hardly looking at the guy in the mirror. During these quiet times, I often finalized in my head what I would say at that morning's Mass, having looked over the three Biblical readings the night before. I usually dressed, wrote in my journal and got into the Chevy wagon to drive over to the sisters' retreat house a mile away. Three of the sisters ran the retreat house.

Another, Sister Ruth, provided religious education at Fort Benning. Sister Ann served as Post Mistress of the little post office on our property. Four sisters taught in our school and helped with our church.

As I drove down the dirt road, avoiding each pot hole, I would pass the Howards' cabin. Priests, brothers and sisters would drive by, looked over at the run-down shack and make remarks like, "God, they sure look poor. How the hell can they stay in that place?" I knew the Howards were struggling and doing the best they could. I was pleased that their children were doing so well in school. Mr. and Mrs. Howard were friendly and always attended PTA meetings. The whole family seemed loving and good. Mr. Howard worked in a warehouse at Fort Benning, and Mrs. Howard was a maid at the Officers Club. Dorothy, the older teen-age girl, waited tables, attended college and was taking instructions to become a Catholic.

The retreat house, with its beautiful floors and arched glass ceiling, was elegant and inviting. I would walk in and go directly to the sacristy, where the priest robes for Mass. The white starched alb went over my black habit, followed by the rope cincture around my middle, then the green stole, and finally the green chasuble covering all the other robes.

I pulled a cord ringing a little bell to announce the beginning of Mass, and the sisters began singing the entrance hymn. After, I began, "In the name of the Father and of the Son and of the Holy Spirit..."

The wall in back of the altar was glass, allowing a beautiful view of the woods. One of the early Trinitarian sisters had inherited these thousand-plus acres that made up the old Mott Plantation. The property swept all the way down to the Chattahoochee River.

After Mass, I jumped back into my car and went back to the refectory to eat a breakfast prepared by Corine or Leila Mae. I was always uneasy about the idea of housekeepers tending to my needs. I never got used to such luxuries. And I was ashamed that the order paid them only $18 per week for more than 40 hours of work. But the women were always pleasant and engaging.

The main cook was Corine. I was surprised one day when she said, "Father, may I come see you sometime?"

"Sure, Corine, when is good for you?"

We decided to meet right after breakfast. Corine came into my office. "Father, I would like to be a Catholic," she said.

I had not expected to hear this from her. Corine agreed to come to Catholic information sessions that would lead to baptism and confirmation. Though her brother was a Baptist preacher, she said she felt called to Catholicism. Her family members rejoiced with her, happy to see she had found something that made her feel closer to God.

Her mother, Leila Mae, sometimes told the story of seeing the first car come down muddy, bumpy Highway 165. She called out in amazement to all within earshot, "Elijah is coming in his chariot! Praise the Lord! It's the end of the world!"

People from the back roads and cabins starting running toward the highway, shouting, screaming and praying.

It's a story that some of the priests would tell and retell to seminarians with great delight when she wasn't around, using exaggerated accents and wearing condescending smiles. In their minds, these hard-working, God-fearing adults were mere children. Maybe they weren't racists, but I bridled when I heard them joking at someone else's expense.

I addressed these and other derogatory remarks directly, as the Religious Superior. I told the brothers and the priests how hurtful and damaging such comments could be, not just to black people who might overhear them, but to us as religious men. While I couldn't dictate what they thought, I did manage to control what they said.

It was one of my few edicts as Superior, and not at all the way I preferred to spend my time and energy. Some priests thought I should be spending more of my time that way, offering more guidance on what they should do or say. But I wanted the life of a priest, not an overseer.

My days were filled with counseling sessions, visits to the school and visits from parishioners. I also was involved in the area's NAACP and spent a couple of days a week at the historically black Tuskegee Institute, working with community leaders on projects aimed at improving African-American communities and attaining equality. At night, I fell into my bed, usually exhausted but fulfilled, content to have each priest rule his own life.

CHAPTER 21

AT HOLY TRINITY, WE DRANK spring water and ate straight-off-the-vine vegetables. We rested beneath lovely magnolias, strong oaks and tall pines. The parishioners often picnicked on church grounds. Children played in open fields. In many ways, life was idyllic.

But, of course, there was also the harsh poverty and ravages of segregation. The signs of it were everywhere, in the impetigo on the children's legs, in the ramshackle cabins, in the stooped backs of 75-year-old women dragging axes to chop wood, in the buckets that carried water from a quarter mile away.

Always, in the interactions between black people and white people, a bit of racial tension lay just beneath the surface. It was painful for me to see the wariness on the faces of some black people when I drove up to their houses to talk about community needs.

Eventually in my exploration of Russell County, I came across Hurtsboro, on the western border. I had seen it on the map, but had never heard any priests or brothers talk about it. I caught sight of a stately, red brick home enclosed by what seemed to be miles of clean white fencing that kept in half a dozen grazing horses. A guesthouse of ample dimension was connected to it.

I continued driving and came to a group of modest but well-kept frame homes. The town's commercial section was still standing but had seen better days. There was a pharmacy, a dry goods store, a bank, a grocery store and a couple of restaurants. Empty shops dotted the street. The town looked bleak and nearly deserted.

A few blocks farther and another right turn brought me to yet another residential area. I passed house after house, one seemingly more decrepit than the next. I drove in another direction and came to another cluster of homes, larger but dilapidated. Black children played in the front yards or in the roadway. Grandmas and grandpas sat on the porches. Once in a while, someone would return my wave. Mostly, I received downcast glances. Some went back into their houses, and some even closed their shutters.

They probably saw me as just another white man in the neighborhood, selling something, collecting money, or looking for sex in some form.

Hurtsboro was small, even by Alabama standards. But it was evident there was a large black population. As I continued my driving excursion, I came across a handsome new building at the end of the main street – the Hurtsboro Clinic. I parked and went up to the building. It was locked up tight. I surmised that it was closed for the day. Seeing this nice building made me feel better, suggesting that Hurtsboro had something modern other than that one stately mansion.

As I circled back, I saw a man I recognized. Slowing the car and opening the window, I called out, "Hey, Mose Jordan, how are you?" I was smiling broadly. Mose had very black skin, a strong build and was of medium height. We had become friends during meetings at Tuskegee Institute. The great Booker T. Washington founded that impressive institution for African Americans. The equally distinguished George Washington Carver taught and conducted his famous research on crops there. Mose and I were part of SEASHA, the Southeast Alabama Self Help Association, an organization that gave assistance to the poor through credit unions, feeder pig projects, housing programs and more.

"Hey, Father. How are you doing? What are you doing way out here?" Mose asked.

I stopped the car, got out and we shook hands in the middle of the street.

"I didn't know you lived here, Mose. Golly, sometime I would like to learn more about this place and have you show me around."

Mose quickly said, "How 'bout now? I got time. You got time?"

I did, so the tour commenced.

"This is my house. My brother lives with his family right there," he said, pointing to a modest home nearby. "My momma lives there," he said, pointing to a smaller home.

I began to tease him, "Mose, you and your family must own the whole town!"

He smiled. "No, we have our little places here, but Mrs. Jones, the rich lady who owns the big house with the horses and white fences you saw as you came in, owns most of the town."

Then his smile disappeared. "And that's the truth. Well, it's mostly true. She owns 33,000 acres, and she owns the bank and most all the buildings downtown. She owns the lumber company down the road, too."

He talked more about the town, the local politics. Clearly, Hurtsboro had many issues that needed to be addressed. I knew that he wanted to improve conditions for black people in the town, to add resources that could help the community. That's why he attended the meetings at Tuskegee. He knew that I knew how to see a project through to completion.

"Talk to me, Mose, what does the community need?" We talked tossed around various ideas, from a credit union to schools.

When it was time for me to go, we decided to get together again to strategize. "We can meet every week," I told him.

"Really, Father?"

"We can do it, really," I replied.

Over the next weeks, I drove out to Hurtsboro and began working with Mose. He introduced me to situations and people. We would meet at his home and discuss issues, or drive in the neighborhood, get out and talk with his friends and family. We couldn't talk at the restaurant, of course. Blacks were served only at the back window.

At the end of one of our conversations, I said, "Mose, do you want to get started on a project? We won't just dance; we'll *do* something."

Mose smiled and replied with his firm and steady voice, "We're ready. This is our life!"

I was excited that he had invited me to help. I didn't want us to do anything foolish that would hurt the black community or the community in general. I wanted to avoid publicity. I had seen such projects blow up dozens of times into bitterness and failure. We settled on a preschool program. A preschool program would help the area's children succeed in school, which would be an investment in the long-term improvement of the area, and would be very non-threatening. Everyone in Hurtsboro, black and white, would understand the need for it. It was a small start, but it was move meant to help empower the black community.

Where would we start? We needed a place. There were many empty buildings. Maybe we could rent one, I thought. I suggested that we talk to the woman who owned most of the town, Mrs. Jones.

"I can't ask her," Mose quickly said. "She ain't gonna talk to me." He wasn't afraid. He just knew she wouldn't talk to him.

I called my friend, attorney Jack Miller, in Phenix City. He and his law partners were very connected. I told him of our plans and asked if he knew Mrs. Jones. Jack told me that his partner was her attorney. He would ask him to talk to her and arrange a meeting.

Some days later, an appointment was set up. With this type of introduction, all would go fine, I thought. I drove up to the grand estate of Mrs. Jones confident I would be able to rent a small empty storefront for the new preschool program. I rang the bell, and a black maid answered the door. I could hear the fierce growls of a couple of German shepherds. A voice from another room said, "Hush." And then, "Lilly, please put the dogs outside."

Soon a woman, age 60 or so, entered the room. She appeared genteel and refined. We sat. For a few minutes, we made small talk centering on mutual acquaintances. We chatted about how successful her deceased husband had been, and she told me a little about her children. Then I said, "Mrs. Jones, would you help me start a preschool? As you know, many poor children need extra help in school, but we need a place to begin. I am not asking for money or anything free, just a chance to rent one of your empty buildings."

"Father," Mrs. Jones said, "I really don't think we need a preschool for the children. All the children I know get what they need.

"Besides," she said, rising from her seat, "I don't have any buildings open at this time. I'm sorry."

The way she said it, while standing up, I could see that this was the end of the conversation and the end of my visit. She was dismissing me, it was clear. Mrs. Jones didn't see any need for improving education. I'm sure she thought exactly as we did – one thing would lead to another. Start with a little preschool and, before you know it, more black people would look for more opportunities to start businesses in Hurtsboro.

My heart sank as I drove out of the driveway. I had talked to others with the same attitude, and would meet more in the course of my lifetime, but it was still disappointing.

I went back to Mose Jordan and told him what Mrs. Jones had said. "She said all the children here are well taken care of in school. Can you believe that?" I said.

Mose smiled. "Father, I knew what she was gonna say before you went, but it's good you found out for yourself."

I told him I knew she might not be open exactly, but I didn't expect her to be so closed.

"Father, her husband was a ticket agent at the railroad. Before he died, he would lend money to people down on their luck and get them to sign papers. If they didn't pay, he'd take over their land. I'm talking just a month late on a couple hundred dollars! Then he kept getting more and more 'til he owned everything around here."

I was being educated to the facts of life in Hurtsboro. Mose continued, "You know the clinic you passed down the street? Mrs. Jones and the board refused federal funds because they would have had to let us use the place. They closed the clinic. They said they didn't want colored to go there.

"It just ain't right," he said. "They can go to Columbus to good doctors, but we can't."

Neither of us was ready to up on the preschool idea. We needed to get creative. There was an old shack across the street from Mose's house. It had a large yard with a chain link fence around it. The shack looked terrible, and the yard was filled with old tin cans and bottles with grass and weeds growing three or four feet high. There were several large pecan trees in the yard.

"Mose, who owns that place?" I asked. "It's a big area, and we could fix it up and begin a preschool."

"A lady in Jersey. She lives up there now."

"Do you know how we could get in touch with her?" I asked.

Mose smiled, "Yes, Father. She's my auntie."

I was beginning to get excited. We went to look at it.

"Would you write her and ask if we could rent the place for $25 a month? It's not much, but we could clean up the whole yard and repair the shack. It has four large rooms and a fenced-in yard, just perfect for a preschool. We will rent it for two years and then we can talk about where we go from there. The rent will pay the taxes, and she will have a nice place in return."

Mose wrote to his aunt, and she agreed. We signed no contract.

I knew a carpenter from the Phenix City NAACP. When I told him of our plans to begin a preschool, he said he would work on the shack himself, beginning the next day. All we would have to do is pay for the materials.

The renovation was about halfway finished, and we had cleared much of the junk off the lot, when one night I got a call from Father Roger, a priest friend from Kentucky. "Do you have some time to talk?" he asked.

"Yes, go ahead, Roger. What is it?"

He always was one to quickly get to the point. "My sister is the head sister in the emergency room in the hospital in Gadsden and she would like to practice rural medicine among the poor. Would you talk with her?" Roger asked.

"Rog, give her my phone number, and I will be glad to talk to her."

I didn't know why a sister who was probably slated to become the administrator of a large hospital one day would want to come and work in rural Alabama. But, if she wanted to, she would be a great asset, I thought. I wondered where the money would come from to support her and how she would adjust to such different work.

When Sister Audrey called, we talked for a long time. I listened very intently to her talk about her hopes, her dreams and her plans. I asked what she would need for support, financially, emotionally and in other ways I couldn't even anticipate.

After we had been talking for a while, I said, "Sister, in addition to doing rural nursing around Holy Trinity, would you also consider beginning a clinic in an oppressed rural town that has much potential but has never set eyes on a Catholic sister? We were going to begin a preschool there. But, with your generous offer to come, it may be best to begin a clinic."

"Father, I can't believe it. It would be a wonderful opportunity. I would love it!" Sister Audrey said.

This was even better than I could have hoped for. I needed to talk to Mose, but knew he would be ecstatic. Sister Audrey and I decided to talk more later. "If we can agree on the terms, we can go forward," I told her.

This was the simple beginning of our work in Hurtsboro. I was happy that we had been flexible, able to see an opportunity and grab it. Sister came. We bought the land and built a new clinic. Then we built a community center and began Montessori classes for the children.

Eventually, the local black funeral director was elected to the city council. And slowly but surely, change came to Hurtsboro.

CHAPTER 22

PEOPLE CALLED HIM COLONEL FRED. He served as an attorney in the Army Judge Advocate General's Corps, assigned the unpleasant job of trying to defend German war criminals at the Nuremberg Trials. The world could not condemn the men who committed the atrocities of World War II without competent legal defense, and he was chosen as one of those who would argue on their behalf. His wife Mary told me that the job sickened him and that he probably never recovered from it.

Fred was a wealthy, gentle Southern boy, educated and distinguished. When he left the Army, he came back to rural Alabama with his lovely wife. All the priests and brothers knew the couple.

They owned thousands of acres in nearby Hatchechubee, Alabama. Mary was Catholic. She received a lot of attention from the priests and brothers, who often praised her, saying she was kind, intelligent, generous, and oh, yes, very beautiful. They said she never flaunted her wealth, a quality that made her even more attractive. She extended kindness to the black people of the mission, and they extended their friendship to her. She was also well loved and respected by the white people of the area.

During my student days at Holy Trinity, I paid little attention to Mary and the Colonel. I didn't know them, but righteously dismissed them as rich white folk. Besides, they got plenty of attention from the other priests. By the time I started work as pastor and superior of Holy Trinity, the Colonel had died from emphysema, and Mary lived alone. Others, like Thelma and Paul Anthony, often encouraged me to get to know her better.

One day after school, Thelma said to me, "Father, Mary was talking to me the other day, and she said she was glad that you were the pastor here at Holy Trinity. She said that she wants to talk to you but is afraid that you don't like her."

It hurt me to hear this from Thelma. I had never meant to be rude to Mary and was sorry she felt that way. Then later that week, one of the nuns asked me, "Father, would you talk to Mary? She really has something she wants to discuss. I don't know what it is."

Again, I felt ashamed of myself. I decided to call Mary that evening.

Mary said, "Oh, Father, how are you tonight? I know you stay so busy, and I don't want to bother you when you could be resting."

"You aren't a bother, Mary. I'm happy to talk with you."

Mary continued, "Father, would you have time to see me? I can wait for whenever is good for you. It probably isn't so important. But, if you have time, I would like to see you."

I could hear in her voice that she was anxious. I agreed to meet her the next day at 11 a.m.

The next morning, there was a knock at my office door. Mary was about 20 years older than I, but she looked much younger than her age. Her hair was dark with wisps of gray. She wore classy clothes and jewelry. She smiled meekly. When she entered the room, I faintly detected an expensive perfume.

"Good morning, Father. Thank you for taking time to see me. If you're busy, I can come back."

I offered her a cup of coffee, and she accepted.

Mary held the cup, stared at me, then broke down into tears. She reached for her tissues. She wiped her eyes, and some of her makeup became a little messy.

"I'm so sorry, Father. I didn't mean to cry. I'm just wasting your time," she said.

"No, Mary," I said. "It's not a waste of my time. It's good to see you. I realize we don't know each other well, but be at peace. It's often hard to talk to another person about personal things. The one thing I can give you is that I will not discuss you with anyone else. I will not betray your confidence. Just take your time."

"Oh, thank you," she said. "This is so terrible, and it hurts so much."

"It's Ok, Mary," I said. "Whatever it is, it's OK."

She finally got this much out: "You know that I help Father Mark in Twin Springs every week? I count the collection and do the church's books."

"Yes, Mary."

"You know that he's had a drinking problem for so long. The order has always been down on him. He has always been stationed in very lonely and poor places. These past few years have been better for him. He's gotten away from drinking. He's made friends. There are people nearby with whom he plays golf or cards and talks."

"That's good," I said, knowing quite a bit about Father Mark. "I'm glad he's doing better."

"No, Father," Mary said. "That's the point. He isn't doing better anymore. He and I have gotten too close."

She started to cry again. "I'm such a terrible person. I've hurt him. He's the kindest man I've ever met. He is so good to everyone. And I've hurt him. I'm terrible."

I felt sorry for all the years I had prejudged her because of her wealth. I could feel her pain and anguish.

Mary was still hesitating.

"Mary, I know that this must be very difficult. Just take your time. Does he know you're talking to me?"

"Yes, he suggested it," she said, tears flowing off her cheeks onto her blouse and skirt.

"It's OK," I said. "Take your time. You're safe here."

Mary continued, "Father, I don't think you understand when I say we've gotten too close."

"I probably don't understand fully," I said. "Only you walk in your shoes. I do know that Mark is a very good and caring person, and you are a very caring person. It's just something that happens. I realize that this is complicated.

"I don't think it's bad to love other people. You are alone now with Fred gone. Father Mark has always been lonely and has been treated badly by the order."

Whether the relationship between them was sexual or not, I frankly didn't care and did not pry for details. I knew, listening to her talk, that I was in a situation where I was suddenly both the church authority and confessor.

"He has struggled with drinking. Now, he is away from alcohol, and that's positive," I said, not sure where to take the conversation.

After an awkward pause, I said, "Mary, first let me assure you that I will help you and Father in any way I can, and I will not betray your confidence." I didn't want to give some cheap words of advice. I told her they could and would work it out themselves.

"Both of you can guide me in what you need from me," I said. "Personally, I'm glad you are there for one another. I think that you and he should think and talk about this yourselves. Whatever decision you make, be assured that I will help you both, and no one else will find out about it. Please be at peace."

"Thank you, Father," she said. "This has been so helpful. I feel I can breathe again. I will talk to him."

"Please call me," I said. "You're a wonderful person and many people love you. Tell him not to hesitate to call if he needs to talk."

Some might have condemned Mary and Father Mark. But entering religious life doesn't mean that you suddenly don't have the same needs and desires as other people.

It's a predicament that many priests – and those who care about them – find themselves in. I could have easily found myself in the same situation. The priesthood can be so isolating. You sometimes long for intimacy, for someone who will love you and understand you and share the journey through life with you.

Certainly, God can help you with this struggle. But I question any priest or bishop who says he doesn't wrestle with celibacy.

I never heard from Father Mark. Not long after Mary's visit, he was transferred. He died soon after, of cancer, I believe. Mary went to live near her daughter and grandchildren in Texas. Until her death, she would call me several times a year. She continued this even after I left the priesthood. We never really discussed in more detail the relationship she shared with Father Mark. I can only hope that both of them were at peace with their decisions.

CHAPTER 23

THEY KNOCKED ON MY FRONT door one day in 1969.

John, originally from Pennsylvania Dutch country, was a soldier stationed at Fort Benning. Evelyn came from a family right up the road. John was a white college grad, a paratrooper who had finished Officers Training School. Evelyn was black, had an eighth-grade education and worked as a cook at Fort Benning. As fate would have it, her mother cleaned the officers' quarters.

One night, John gave the mother a ride home when her car broke down on the base. Evelyn was at home when they pulled up. She thanked the officer for seeing her mother safely home, and the two struck up a conversation. They talked for a long time that night. Then they met up again. Over time, they began to fall in love.

It was dark and raining when they showed up at my place. I opened the door and was a little taken aback. Mixed couples were a rare sight. I recognized Evelyn, though I didn't know her family well. I would often pass their weather-beaten cabin near the road and see the many children playing in the front yard. There was usually a junk car or two on cement blocks in the back yard. I would wave to the children and occasionally stop to say hello.

"Come in," I said, wondering why they were there.

Evelyn spoke first, "Father, I hear that you're nice, and you always greet our family when you go to town. So, John and I would like to talk with you."

Then John said, "I am being transferred to Germany, and I love Evelyn, and we want to be married. We know that everyone will tell us that we are wrong, and that no preacher or justice of the peace will marry us. The chaplains at Fort Benning will not marry us.

Please, will you help us? We have our families' permission, and we have known each other for a year and a half."

Evelyn continued, "I know I'm colored and John is white, and he has more learning than me. But, Father, I am not dumb. My daddy and momma don't have much, but we are a loving family. I love John and will be a good wife. John loves me and never has been bad to me. He isn't ashamed of me in public. We would like to be married."

They sat down, and we talked about every aspect interracial marriage, positive and negative, not dodging raw and important issues. While the differences between John and Evelyn were obvious, their love also was obvious.

"When do you go to Germany?" I asked.

"In two weeks," John replied. "I can't take Evelyn with me then. But, if we are married, I can send for her."

We talked, and I thought for a long time. It was Saturday evening. I told them to come by the following Wednesday for my answer.

Wednesday evening came, bringing another visit from John and Evelyn. It was clear that their love and determination was strong. A pastor in Mississippi once told me that he never interrogated couples who came to him and wanted to be married. "If they seem to have thought through their decision, why should I stand in the way? I have never been able to tell which marriages will work and which will not." I called to mind his words.

"I will marry you Saturday, if you wish," I said. "But I have to admit, it is quick, and I could have my head handed to me. Do you realize that?"

They nodded.

"You have to get a license," I continued, "and I don't know how to do that."

They both smiled. John said he knew how to get a license. "Father, we know that this is different," he said. "But it's better than just having an affair or just having a light-skinned baby with no father. We know it won't be easy."

I married John and Evelyn that Saturday with another couple present as witnesses. After the ceremony, he flew off to Germany, and she joined him some months later.

I heard nothing from them for a while. Now and then, I would stop by Evelyn's parents' home for a chat and hear that the couple was doing fine. Before long, I heard that they were expecting their first child.

Then I got a frantic call from John one morning at around 3 a.m. He was still in Germany.

"Father," he sobbed. "Will you help me, please? Evelyn is dead. She died giving birth to our baby. She had cancer, and no one knew about it until the baby came. I want to bring her home to bury her. Will you help me?"

"Yes, John, you know I will. How is the baby?"

"The baby is a beautiful, healthy boy," John replied. "My mother is flying over tomorrow and will help me with him."

"All of us at Holy Trinity will help. If you and your family need to, we will have a Mass and service here."

We continued to talk for a few minutes, then we said goodbye, agreeing to stay in touch about arrangements.

The next day I received a call from John's mother in Pennsylvania. She was a professional woman in a high-powered position. She was thankful for the kindness I had shown to the couple. She swore to commit herself and her resources to making sure that the child would be well taken care of. They would all live together in her home.

The funeral Mass for Evelyn was quite touching. The choir was made up of nearly 300 children. They sang about love and joy and saying goodbye. Mostly black mourners came, overflowing the church by several hundred. It was a new experience for most of them to see a white man crying over the death of a black woman.

John walked up the aisle with his mother. In his arms, he held a beautiful infant, wrapped in a lovely blue blanket.

CHAPTER 24

PERHAPS NO ONE PLAYED A bigger role than Thelma Miller in helping me gain acceptance in the black community. I met Thelma during a summer stay at Holy Trinity when I was 22 years old. When I came back to Holy Trinity as the pastor and superior, she welcomed me into her circle.

During a time of profound racial injustice, Thelma looked for ways to improve the lives of her African-American neighbors. She recognized that I wanted to help in the fight against intolerance and bigotry.

Though surrounded by poverty, Thelma was not poor. Her father, Hamp Miller, was a timber cruiser, which, in the 1950s and '60s was an unlikely profession for a black man in rural Alabama. Her grandfather was a white man. In all, I think there were nine children in her family, every one of them gifted.

At one time, Thelma had wanted to become a nun. But she was turned away because, as a child, she had rheumatic fever and it damaged her heart. Maybe her desire to join a religious community is one of the reasons she showed me so much empathy. Here I was, white, raised in eastern Wisconsin, trying to fit in.

Thelma paved the way for me by speaking of me as not just a nice priest, but someone to be trusted.

Sister Julian was one of the many people I met through Thelma. Before Julian joined the Vincentian Sisters of Charity, she and Thelma had gone to high school together at Mother Mary Mission in Phenix City. They were the best of friends. As the years passed, Sister Julian and I became close friends.

Julian was of medium height and on the heavy side. She had a wide gap in her upper front teeth. She had penetrating eyes and a ready smile that could vanish in a second if she found herself in a hostile environment. She worked long and hard, mostly in Montgomery. Almost everywhere she went, she was the only black nun. Sometimes, she suffered cruelty because of that. Sister used me for spiritual direction and private counseling many times in her life.

One night in 1968, after Martin Luther King Jr. was killed, she called me. "Father Emil, would you pick me up tomorrow night here at the City of St. Jude and take me to the special service they are having in Selma? Julian Bond is going to be the speaker."

"Sister, what time does it start and what time will it end?" I asked.

"It starts at about 8 p.m., and it ends when it's over. There's a supper after the service," she said. Then with a laugh, she added, referring to the mostly black crowd that would be attending, "You know us folk aren't going to be in any hurry."

"OK, Sister," I groaned. "How could I say no to you, even though I'll probably be getting back to Holy Trinity at 3 a.m. and I have to be up at 5:30. You're going to kill me, but I do want to hear Julian Bond myself."

The next day, later in the afternoon, I gassed up the car at Holy Trinity and took the back roads through Seale and Tuskegee to Montgomery. Julian came out of the convent bursting with energy, excited at the prospect of hearing the other Julian.

"Hi, Father, it's great you can drive me to this program. My superiors wouldn't let me go alone".

"I'm happy you called and grateful for this opportunity," I replied, even though I was already dead tired from a long day of work.

Sister Julian was idealistic and dedicated. As we drove the 50 miles over to Selma, we talked about many things.

Then she got on the subject of her early days as a nun and how she was treated. "I was sometimes tripped going up to communion," she said. She began to cry.

"That's why it is so good you are taking me to this gathering tonight. I can sit with my brothers and sisters, be comfortable and listen to Julian Bond."

In Selma, there was a large, mostly black crowd gathered at the church. I spotted another white priest, a friend of mine, Father Don. He barely spoke to me before turning away. Later, I said to him, "Hey, you hardly acknowledged me when Julian and I came in."

As it turned out, Father Don was trying his best to lay low and blend in. The last thing he needed was to be standing next to another white man. "Since Martin was killed, I have been afraid of being insulted because I'm white," he said. "Last night, I was on a program and another panelist, a black man, said, 'I ain't gonna be on the same program with a motherfucking white man.' And he walked off the stage. I felt terrible."

"Don, don't take it personally," I said. "Many black people are angry, but you and I live and work daily in the black community. We know of the injustices. Some black people may not like us, and that's OK. We do what we do because we believe in justice."

I didn't mean to preach to him. He was hurt and frightened. But these angry, violent times had everyone on edge. Some African Americans were struggling to not paint the whole white race with the same brush. I often had to remind myself that, even with the endorsement of Thelma and others, some would view me with suspicion. But that did not relieve me, or Father Don, of our responsibility to join the fight for equality.

The program was filled with prayers, songs and speeches. Finally, Julian Bond walked to the podium. Bond had been a student at Morehouse and was a founding member of the Student Nonviolent Coordinating Committee. Just a few years earlier, after the Voting Rights Act was passed, he had been one of eight black people elected to the Georgia's House of Representatives. The House had refused to seat him because he backed SNCC's stand against the Vietnam War. Only after the Supreme Court got involved was Bond eventually allowed to take office. I had admired him for a long time.

There was a big dinner in the church basement after his talk was over. Sister Julian and I went downstairs, where the line was so long that we gave up on getting supper. We milled around, visiting with people. After a long while, we gravitated to the kitchen, hoping to get some leftover morsel and be on our way.

The women who were cooking and serving spotted us. Julian was in her sister's habit and I in my clerical collar. They called us over, cleared off a table and sat us down. Soon, another man came through the kitchen door, not able to get a seat in the dining room, and the ladies sat him down next to me. "Hi," he said. "I am Julian Bond."

I couldn't believe my good fortune. The three of us talked and talked. I was suddenly in no hurry at all. He could not have been more personable. Finally remembering that we still had a long drive back, Sister Julian and I excused ourselves. It was late when I dropped her at the front door of the convent.

"Father, thanks so much," she said. "You're great. I had a wonderful time and feel like a new person."

I returned the gratitude, "Thank you for asking me to go and for the trust you have in me. And thank you for the opportunity to meet and talk with Julian Bond. It was a beautiful evening. I am very inspired."

As I pulled out of the driveway of the City of St. Jude, headed toward lonely, rural roads, it was about 2:30 a.m. I was exhausted, but lived for these moments, when I gathered with like-minded people.

Julian and I lost touch for a while, but reconnected. I officiated at her funeral Mass at Mother Mary Mission in Phenix City in the mid-1980s. Like so many others, she died of cancer at a young age. Sister Julian worked so tirelessly for so long with little support from others. To this day, she is still an inspiration to me.

CHAPTER 25

MUCH OF MY ON-THE-JOB TRAINING came from the nuns who taught in the school and served the parish. These sisters demonstrated patience and goodness when I was immature and ignorant.

Not long after I arrived at Holy Trinity, Sister Renee was named principal of St. Joseph's School. I didn't know her, but some of the nuns did. Before she ever stepped foot onto our grounds, the other sisters were singing her praises.

Sister Mary opened the door to my office the day the letter arrived announcing Renee's appointment. Smiling, she said, "Renee is coming to be our new principal! It's wonderful. She's so intelligent and funny. She'll help us so much."

Sister Mary was 4 feet 10 inches and a dynamo, full of energy. Her large brown eyes flashed everywhere, never missing a thing. That she was ecstatic about Sister Renee's arrival said much. Mary was dedicated to liberation issues, meaning she, too, believed the Church had an obligation to help make life better for the poor and to change unjust social and political conditions.

She and Sister Elizabeth would often drive with me to other African-American churches in the county. We would show films about how to start credit unions and other community development projects. This was after they had spent all day in the classroom and performed chores at the convent.

Sister Elizabeth, too, expressed her happiness about Renee. Sister Elizabeth was about 5 feet, 10 inches. I looked up to her, not just in an inspirational sense, but physically, too.

"Father, Sister Renee will know what we need to do, and she will help us accomplish it, not just make rules," said Sister Elizabeth, her red Irish face glowing. A few tears of joy rolled down her cheeks.

Before long, Sister Laurie joined us. Sister Laurie outworked all of us in the school and church. The teenage boys and girls loved her, even though she stayed on them about their grades. She smiled upon hearing the news of Sister Renee's appointment.

I had found out about Renee's appointment only a couple of hours earlier. I would've been thankful for anyone the order sent, but the news that it was to be Renee made everyone so happy that it gave me much hope.

The sisters and I talked for some time, full of expectation.

When they turned to leave, Sister Elizabeth stopped and asked, "Father, may I see you privately for a few minutes?"

After the others had left, Sister said, "Father, I have a problem, and I want your help. If you don't want to help, it will be OK. But I have to ask you."

"Sister, just tell me how I can help, and I will try," I assured her.

"Father, we do not have any money to buy private things, and all sisters need private things. Frankly, I sometimes smoke cigarettes. I smoked before going into the convent and have had to give them up. I get so tense sometimes. And, while I do not wish to do anything wrong, I just need to have a cigarette once or twice a week."

"Sister, how can I help you?" I asked. "I don't make the rules. And, you know, smoking isn't healthy for you."

Sister Elizabeth looked down. "I'm sorry I asked you. I only smoke one or two cigarettes a week. I don't think that's bad."

I felt ashamed. "Sister, I'm sorry," I said. "I need to listen better. I have no opinion about whether you smoke or not. Bishops, priests and brothers smoke, so why can't you? I trust your judgment, I really do. I was just expressing my concern for your health."

Sister Elizabeth looked at me and smiled. "Thanks so much for understanding. Even if you don't, you've been very nice."

"Sister, before you go. Tell me, do the other sisters have *no* money for personal things?"

"That's right, even the elderly sisters."

"How much do you get paid?" I asked.

"Father, we receive $75 a month on a nine-month basis, and the money goes directly to the running of the convent, and we send some to the Motherhouse. We don't have any free money for our own personal needs."

I understood the vow of poverty in religious orders fairly well, but this still seemed ridiculous. While it was not my place to control how the sisters' community worked, they labored long and hard for the school. It seemed to me that, while those who held the power in these orders had money for their own needs, they turned very strict and frugal when doling out cash. I could at least help the nuns at Holy Trinity.

"If I gave some money to each of the sisters each month for her personal needs, whatever those needs are, do you think that would be helpful?"

"Father, it would be wonderful, so wonderful. Then we wouldn't have to ask for things that are private."

"Sister, I will do that each month. I will talk to Sister Renee when she arrives in a couple of days. We will arrange for better pay and have some money for personal needs."

I stood to leave, headed to another meeting, and she said, "Father, where will you get the money for all of this? The other priests always say that they can't afford to pay us much or even get us a decent car. Our car has no insurance so we can only drive from our house to the school, and we can see the road through the large hole in the floor of the car."

I wasn't sure exactly sure where I'd get the money, but I knew I would. "Sister, I worry about many things in life, but I don't worry about money. For now, you will just have to trust me."

A couple of days later, about 9 in the morning, I heard a loud knock on my office door. A sister came in, smiling. "Hi, Father. I'm Sister Renee."

Sister Renee wore a black dress that went below her knees, a small white collar and a pin. Trinitarian sisters didn't don veils and long habits like Franciscan and Dominican sisters.

I rose from my chair and walked over to her. "It's wonderful to meet you, and we're so happy to have you as our new principal. Several people have told me how good you are."

Sister answered quickly with a little laugh, "Don't believe them, Father. I'm so unorganized that you will need to send for extra help."

Sister Renee was of medium height and weight and wore rimless glasses. She was pretty with light brown hair and walked quickly wherever she went.

I continued, "Sister, you will do just fine. When you get settled, we can talk. Just let me know when you are ready. I really am happy that you're here, and I want to help with the school. There are so many needs."

Sister confessed that she had some anxiety.

"I know you'll do well, and we'll help," I said. "Please be at peace."

Sister smiled and said, "Thanks, Father. I want to do my best."

Little did I know how much she would teach me as the months and years went by.

She started to walk away, then stopped. "Father, I can talk now. The teachers are in the school with the children."

"Fine," I said. "One of the first things is that I want you to take these keys. They are to the blue Chevy station wagon. It's new, and it's for you and the sisters in the school. Would you find out what sisters are paid nationally? I will increase your pay to that, and each school sister will receive another $25 a month for personal expenses. This is only fair. If we are unjust to the sisters, the lay teachers and workers here at Holy Trinity, I don't know how we can speak of social justice anywhere else."

The car that I gave her was mine. I was pretty sure I could get another from a priest who was leaving the area. And the money for raises came from the order and friends of mine who were quite generous.

Sister Renee looked at me and started to cry. I felt embarrassed. I was just trying to be fair. I remembered my talks at

Catholic University with Sister Monica, who wanted so much to improve conditions for her fellow nuns, often taken for granted and mistreated.

Sister Renee thanked me profusely.

"Father, in the next weeks and months, I will meet with the sisters and teachers, and we will outline what our goals and needs are. Please join us, and we can all work on our most pressing needs together."

"Fantastic, Sister," I replied. "I will be glad to join you and listen to the others."

"Yes, Father, but please bring your ideas. We need to know what you are expecting of us and what your goals are for Holy Trinity."

Then, almost as an afterthought, she said, "Father, what should we do with this note the sisters gave me?"

She gave me the note and I saw some crude scribbling: "Priest, we don't like niggers going to school with white children. Look out cause your place is gonna be burnt."

I knew the letter's author, Zeke Bloom. He had pulled this on the previous priest. He owned a gas station up the road and would shout obscenities at the African American people who came there. He was a bigot, proud and bullying. In full-page ads in the Phenix City newspaper, he asserted that black people were not human. The Phenix City paper was money hungry enough to print Bloom's garbage. Who knows, the newspaper's editors may have even believed it.

The burning of churches and schools, of course, was not unheard of in Alabama in the 1960s. But I knew that the Trinitarians had our buildings at Holy Trinity very well insured.

"Sister, write a letter on our letterhead in my name and tell our friend Zeke to please notify us when he is going to burn our school down. We would not want the children harmed and will get them out. Tell him that we are very heavily insured, and we would build a new brick school with the insurance proceeds. And, of course, the insurance company would start a criminal investigation. Assure him that we will be keeping his letter at our headquarters in Washington, D.C. I will sign the letter when you have it and carry it down to him personally."

I told her not to worry. "Thank you for showing me the letter. Let me worry about these things. You concentrate on the school. I'm sure we'll work wonderfully together."

We did work wonderfully together. Over time, I began to like Renee very much, but kept this to myself. Sometimes, while driving back on lonely dark roads, from meetings in Tuskegee, Mobile or Montgomery, the voice of Percy Sledge would pierce the dark, silent night with his song, "When a Man Loves a Woman." His haunting voice and direct words dug deeply into my soul.

CHAPTER 26

IN THE MIDDLE OF RURAL Alabama, I met a scholar, rebel and soulmate. Sister Renee and I had no plans to run off together in a romantic relationship, but we treasured each other.

"You have such great ideas for the school, for religious life and for the people of this whole area," I would tell her. "It's great to work with you,"

"No, it's you, Father," she'd say. "You put wheels under my crazy ideas and make them real."

"I have another idea for our school, Father," she said to me one day. "I talked it over with Sister Elizabeth and Sister Mary. I also talked to Thelma and the PTA president."

"You probably want a new school," I playfully said.

"Oh, how did you know? I can't believe that you guessed!"

"I'm just kidding, Sister," I said, a bit taken aback.

"I'm not," she said. "You and I have talked so much about our hopes for the children and their parents. We all know that education is the key to liberation for the poor. Father, I've read and studied Maria Montessori and her views of education. What she did for the neglected children of Rome and the world, we can do in Alabama."

She recommended that I read some books. I agreed to, but still couldn't imagine such a massive undertaking.

Sister Renee had no intention of dropping the subject. In the days that followed, we talked more. And I read. Gradually, I began to embrace the idea.

"OK, Sister, we will work to build a new school. We will work together until it's done," I finally said. The moment I said it, I felt exhilarated. The project would make a bold statement about Holy Trinity's values and priorities.

Several months and many meetings later, hundreds of parents crowded into our school cafeteria for a PTA meeting – tall Willie Taylor, with his wife, Gertie Mae; Mrs. P.G. Ford; Mr. James Jones from Crossroads. To some extent, we all knew one another. We had been together in the same room a year ago on the evening Martin Luther King Jr. was killed. Seven of us traveled together to his funeral. I knew where each family lived and had been to most of their homes.

The community's support, of course, was essential if we wanted to build a new school. I pondered the best way to announce our intentions. I greeted the group, then got to the point.

"We all know that we have many lessons to teach and to learn," I said. "We have oppression to overcome, in addition to the learning we must do. We have to be people of belief and hope.

"I have a special announcement to make. We are going to build a new school here at Holy Trinity. It will have the best of teaching materials, and it will be safe, modern and beautiful."

I paused and looked around at the crowd. There were no angry outbursts from people who thought the time and energy could be better spent on another project. Many of the faces wore smiles, so I continued.

"I am aware that many people may not believe that we can do this. I have thought and prayed over this. I have talked long and hard with Sister Renee, each teacher, our PTA president and others. It's time for all of us to be bold and to step out. I ask for your moral support. We can do it. We will do it. Thank you."

Several people raised their hands and asked questions. While a few of the parents might have thought we were aiming too high, it was clear we had the support of the majority.

I talked to members of the General Council of my religious order about raising money for the new school. The order had just built seminaries in Virginia and Maryland and a retreat house for sisters. If they could raise money for seminaries and religious houses, I thought, they could raise a few hundred thousand for a rural elementary school. I received permission to approach an architect.

I called Ted Szutowicz, who had worked with Holy Trinity before. He was excited about the project, but he warned that it would be much more involved than the previous work. "The last building we did together was about 5,000 square feet, and it was a residence. The kindergarten we built was one room with 2,000 square feet," he said. "The new school could end up about 18,000 square feet, a much bigger, more expensive and complicated project. It will take a lot of planning between you, me and the builder."

I told Ted that I had promised the principal and the teachers that they also could have input in plans for the school. They were putting together a list of what they wanted and didn't want in their new building.

The sisters, the teachers, Ted and I met dozens of times. We also involved representatives of the Kettering Foundation, which had partnered with Auburn University to implement a schools program called Individually Guided Education. Some of us took trips to Memphis, Cincinnati, Detroit, Boston and Washington D.C., to visit schools. We wanted to build a facility that was functional and beautiful.

We planned to have an auditorium for children to have plays and other performances. The auditorium would open up to the cafeteria, where overflow crowds could be accommodated. A small chapel was planned for faculty and children. We would have stained glass windows that filtered light into the chapel and auditorium. A large media center would be set up in the middle of our octagon-shaped school, giving each class immediate access. There would be no walls between classrooms and the media center. For the times privacy was needed, there would be folding walls between each classroom. In the event of fire, the whole school could be evacuated in about 30 seconds.

The architect had the plans drawn up, and the project went out for bid. Before long, the school began to take shape.

It was thrilling to see this idea come to life. Sister Renee was even more excited than I was.

In the autumn, a handsomely dressed gentleman pulled his car into the driveway. He got out, walked over to the construction site and started looking around. I went over to him and introduced myself. The man's family had started a foundation in Illinois that had given a large donation for the school. After looking through the partially built school, he turned to me and shook my hand. "Father, our foundation gives a lot of money to many projects like this, but we often don't know if recipients are doing a good job. I'm so proud of this new school and what you're doing. It makes me very happy, and it will make my family happy when I tell them."

It was great to receive positive feedback.

The building was finished in 1971. The superior general from my order came to bless the building. I asked John Brown, my good friend from Tuskegee, to give the keynote address. John had started a nonprofit called the Southeast Alabama Self Help Association, a community development corporation that helps develop affordable housing. He was an influential person in my life who advised and mentored me.

For nearly three decades, the school served the needs of children in the area. But, by the late 1990s, there was a strong feeling among those working in education in the Catholic Church that only schools that could financially support themselves should exist. The school at Holy Trinity was closed.

Raising the funds and building the school was an extraordinarily fulfilling endeavor for me, Sister Renee and everyone involved. We lived on the high of our achievement for a while. But, eventually, Sister Renee began looking around for new challenges. She no longer felt connected to the order and religious life. She wanted to leave the Trinitarians and go for more Montessori training in Italy. I gave her money for travel and to help with tuition. She went on to become an expert in Montessori education.

It was hard to say goodbye to Sister Renee. She was such a driving force at Holy Trinity. But I have always been grateful for our years together, and I understood her need for a fresh start.

Despite the gratifying work with the school and my love for the community, I, too, had started to question if the Trinitarian order still made sense for me.

CHAPTER 27

LOOKING BACK, I CAN SEE that I was exhausted from juggling so many responsibilities in the school, church and community. I also can see that I never really embraced my duties as religious superior.

I didn't want the job, to be truthful. I was 20 years younger than most of the priests and brothers assigned to Holy Trinity, and there were fundamental differences in the way I defined my role and the way they defined it.

As a seminarian, I was always resentful of the heavy-handed way some superiors ruled. Perhaps because I had no interest in climbing the ecclesiastical ladder, my approach was more to "live and let live."

This was not what most of the priests and brothers at Holy Trinity wanted. They were used to top-down management. The superior, in their view, was supposed to focus on religious community life. He decided how the priests would spend their time. He made the money decisions, everything from which priests needed cars and how much to spend on them to whether to buy a new television.

But our community had a bursar, and I was more than happy to delegate financial matters to him. I also felt that making so many decisions about the daily lives of the priests and brothers encouraged an unhealthy dependence.

Some thought I should have been stricter. In the past, the expectation was that everybody would be at daily community prayers at 5:30 sharp. No exceptions. Priests and brothers at Holy Trinity had always eaten meals together and usually watched TV together. I wasn't interested in enforcing the rules. The problem was, many times, I wasn't there. When I finished a long day of prayers, meditation, Mass, counseling sessions, school duties and grounds oversight, it was time for my community work.

America was changing. More African Americans were registered to vote because of the hard-fought battles so many had engaged in. That meant more African Americans were elected to office. Those of us who believed in equal rights turned our attention to finding the best ways to make use of the court decisions and federal regulations that banned discrimination.

I attended local NAACP meetings and, twice a week, community-organizing meetings at Tuskegee Institute, an hour away.

Since my days in the seminary, I've had a proclivity for obsessive focus when I become involved in projects of interest. The civil rights work was stimulating and energizing. And I prided myself on being a doer, not a talker. But the 18-hour workdays simply wore me out. The expectations of the priests and brothers on top of that were too much to handle.

I began to struggle again with anxiety and depression, despite medication, counseling and prayer. At the same time, I was having a harder time overlooking what I perceived as the Church's shortcomings – its unequal treatment of women and gay people and a hierarchy that often ignored the struggles of the oppressed.

Though I was not ready to give up on the priesthood, I came to the conclusion that maybe I was not cut out for life in a religious order, or at least not the Trinitarian order.

In 1975, I requested permission to leave the Trinitarians, an act considered akin to treason. I had hoped to talk it over with the superior general. But instead, he sent Father Joseph, a member of the General Council. There were five priests on the General Council. The priest sent to talk to me was a person I had never gotten along with well.

We met at the airport in Atlanta. Father Joseph seemed to completely disregard my abilities and felt that I didn't have the qualities necessary to be a good priest. He said he thought I didn't fit in, that my priorities were skewed with my work in the black community. The truth was that he hadn't come to help me decide. He wanted to tell me to go. He made it easy.

"I know you want to leave the Trinitarians. I think that's good. I don't think that you're a very good priest, so it's probably for the best. It's probably the will of God."

He was partly right, I thought. It was the will of God. My superiors never seemed comfortable with my focus on the poor and civil rights. We made it official: I would no longer be Father Emil, the Trinitarian. I was Richard Keil again. Still, I wanted to be a priest. My love for God had not waned.

Maybe, just maybe, I thought, I could find others in the Church who viewed my work as important. I wasn't interested in another order. I didn't want to be distracted by life in a religious community. I felt the primary focus should be on serving the people. I decided to contact a bishop in Georgia. It seemed the time was right for me to work as a diocesan priest.

Lessons Along the Way

CHAPTER 28

"'TIS A GOOD DAY, LAD. 'Tis a good day," Father Galvin called to me as he made his way to the kitchen. "Oh, Lad, I'll be putting my porridge in the double boiler before Mass at the convent, and I'll leave the chicken and spinach to boil in a pot."

John Galvin was a youngish 70, with an upbeat nature. He swam every day, and it showed in his solid, athletic build.

I found him easy to live with, which came as a relief. I had prepared myself for the worst. Many of the Irish priests I'd known over the years had been rigid traditionalists. The Ireland John Galvin grew up in was a conservative Catholic stronghold that supplied the world with priests even as the rest of Europe trended more toward secularism. Over the years, I had heard many Irish priests brag about how superior the Irish were at running churches and understanding "real" theology. Often, this pontificating was done with whiskey on their breath.

When I was named pastor of St. Peter Claver in Macon, Georgia, I was thrilled to be assigned to such a diverse, vibrant church. When I was told that the former pastor was to live with me, I was nervous.

Father Galvin quickly showed me I had no cause. In our first days together, I saw him in the church hall with a group of people after Mass. He turned to speak to one young woman. "Oh, Patricia, you are divorced now? God bless you. Are you fine, my dear?"

"Yes, Father," she responded.

"Well, my dear, I know you just divorced. But, in a year or two, find yourself a nice husband. You are too young and too beautiful not to be married. God bless you, my dear."

As antiquated as it sounds, the Catholic Church doesn't permit divorce for valid sacramental marriages. So marrying again is only allowed if the Church determines the union wasn't valid. But Father Galvin offered no judgment about the divorce, only compassion.

He was a straightforward man who taught me much.

"I've seen the Church and America change so much," he told me. "Some things are still old fashioned, don't you know. The bishops are still telling couples not to use birth control. Now what do you think of that? Oh, God almighty, the young think for themselves now. And the blacks do well for themselves now.

"Lad, oh my, the racism used to be so terrible when I was in Africa and in Savannah and here in Macon. The Bishop of Savannah actually wanted missionary priests to work in the black churches. His clergy were too good, too afraid or didn't care to work here at St. Peter Claver."

Father Galvin loved St. Peter Claver. The church had a rich history. For a number of years in the late 1800s, members of the Society of Jesus, or Jesuits, assumed responsibility for saying Mass for Macon's African-American Catholics. But, according to an article in the Savannah Diocese magazine, Southern Cross, the Jesuits decided to pack up and leave when several priests contracted yellow fever. Responding to a request from the diocese's bishop, the Society of African Missions took over the small school and church in the early 20th century. A provincial from that order believed that black Catholics should have their own churches in their own neighborhoods. So, with funding from Mother Katharine Drexel, a Philadelphia heiress who founded Sisters of the Blessed Sacrament for Indians and Colored People, a school, convent and rectory was built on Ward Street in the Pleasant Hill neighborhood.

As a member of the Society of African Missions, Father Galvin had spent many years on that continent before coming to Georgia. He knew many people in Macon and visited all of the black neighborhoods. He would go from house to house, just being friendly, offering prayers, not coming off as preachy.

People would laugh at him because he would often park his car in the middle of the street. Whenever anyone warned him about doing so, he would say others could just drive around it. These were in the days when some black neighborhoods still had dirt streets and no sidewalks.

Father Galvin spent 28 years at St. Peter Claver. We lived together for more than four years. He would say, "Oh, lad, you are doing so well. God bless you. You are the most wonderful priest ever at St. Peter Claver. I have seen great priests, and I have seen terrible priests here."

He had some paternalism in him, like many of us, and would sometimes throw change to children from his room on the second floor. But he was a precious man. He frequently said that all we have is what we give away.

I looked around at his shabby room one day and asked, "Is there anything you would like for your room?"

"Really, Father?" he said.

"Yes, you deserve the basic things you need. Do you get a pension?"

"Oh, lad, the Bishop says the order should pay my expenses, and the order thinks that the diocese should support me, since I worked in the diocese for over 30 years. I get a few dollars from covering parishes in the area on weekends and some weekdays when the regular priests are away."

I shook my head. "Father Galvin, we will give you some money each month. What would you like for you room?"

"Well," he said, "don't you know, I could use a nice chair and a lamp and a rug. I love to read. But don't worry about it, lad. Oh, I'm fine."

"Father, go find the rug, chair and lamp that you want and have it delivered. We can pay for it. You have done so much for so many," I cheerfully responded. The way the Church treats its elderly, sometimes, is pathetic. A rug and a couple of pieces of furniture seemed the least we could do.

One late night in 1980, about 2 a.m., I heard a thump in Father Galvin's room. I got up quickly and opened the door. Father was lying on the floor in his T-shirt and shorts. He had just had what I think was a stroke. I called for an ambulance, and EMTs were at the door in a few minutes. They carried Father down the stairs on a stretcher. In a few seconds, the siren was on, and Father Galvin was off to the hospital. I followed.

He spent some days at Coliseum Hospital. Then the order arranged for him to be transferred to Tenafly, New Jersey. He died a few weeks later. I cleaned out his room and sent his few items to the order and his family. Among his meager belongings were letters from the famous American writer, Flannery O'Connor, who lived not far away in Milledgeville, compilations of Shakespeare's plays, his prayer books, his Bible and a few things that resembled clothes. I cried.

The provincial of the Society of African Missions came to Macon to thank me for taking care of Father Galvin and later sent an official letter of gratitude, which I treasure. I often think of John Galvin, and his mantra: All we have is what we give away.

A St. Peter Claver School scholarship fund is named for him.

CHAPTER 29

THE MAN ON THE OTHER end of the telephone was annoyed. Why, he asked me, would a white man want to open a museum dedicated to African-American achievements? And why would I want to name such a place after Harriet Tubman? My plan just showed how little thought I'd put into the whole idea, he said.

"All she did was escape from slavery with the help of white Yankees," he asserted. "She really never did anything on her own."

Listening to the man, a white lawyer in town, just reaffirmed my opinion that too many people were ignorant of black history. "The point is to educate people, because she did so much on her own," I said. "She returned to the South multiple times helping others to escape. She became a nurse, a guide and a spy for the Union Army. She started a home for the elderly and was a founder of the National

Association of Colored Women. She also worked with the suffrage movement. Maybe you should read a little more history."

We hung up, and, while I never heard from him again, I heard from others like him.

The Tubman Museum had been a long-time dream of mine. Macon – a lovely city, situated in the middle of the state – seemed the perfect place to make it happen. Macon had two interstates running through it, several colleges and strong black leaders. Macon also had a enviable musical heritage that included several well-known and incredibly influential artists, like Little Richard and Otis Redding. They, too, were a part the area's black history.

It was 1981. In the quarter of a century I'd spent pastoring in black churches, I had seen the legacy of slavery and segregation. Too many African Americans were living in poverty in crime-ridden neighborhoods where drug use was rampant and the black pride of the 1960s and 1970s had fallen by the wayside. Starting a museum wasn't just an act of love and appreciation. It was necessary.

Even though race relations had improved significantly over time, and blacks were continually making strides in the economic arena, there were simply too few repositories of black history. Too few museums reminded people of the contributions, and sacrifices, of African Americans; too few centers embraced black culture and portrayed African Americans in a positive light. History books tended to overlook the triumphs of black Americans.

I had visited many of the museums in the country that focused on the African-American experience, and I felt ready – with a lot of help – to add one to the landscape. I had learned so many lessons from the black community, and witnessed so many beautiful moments in the struggle for equality, that it seemed only natural. Plus, unlike some, I had a flexible schedule that allowed me to spend time on the project.

I talked over the idea with some local leaders who were trusted friends, among them Gloria Washington, the principal of Southwest High School; Dr. Bobby Jones, a professor of education at Mercer University; Albert Billingslea, a contractor and county commissioner, and his wife Margaret; Pearlie and John Toliver, a bank vice president and a state government official, respectively. Their words could not have been more encouraging. And they made it clear that they were ready to roll up their sleeves, as well.

The first order of business was to find the right location. Over time, I looked at 15 or so buildings before a friend, real estate professional Holst Beall, called me about a spot on Walnut Street in downtown Macon.

The building was filthy inside. Through the years, it had been a furniture store, a warehouse and a nightclub. The last occupants had kept guard dogs upstairs, and the floors were littered with dirt and dog droppings. The price was $18,000 for half of the building. At first, I found the size to be intimidating. It seemed too large. Still, I could see the potential.

I met with Maureen Walker one night in July to talk it over. At the time, Maureen was director of the Ruth Hartley Mosley Center, a facility in Macon dedicated to uplifting black women. I asked her opinion: Was it the right place? Should I wait?

She looked at me and said, "If you can get it, get it," and rattled off her reasons.

That night, I pondered Maureen's advice. I knew she was right.

Albert Billingslea inspected the property and assured me that it was sound. I ended up not buying half the building, but the whole thing. I made the down payment and personally signed for the loan, confident that others would contribute. And they did. Rabbi Ron Goldstein helped us to obtain funds from the Porter Foundation. A friend, Suzanne Engel, had close ties to the Grassmann Trust and helped us secure a large grant. Many, many others contributed either money or their time and skills toward the project.

Gradually, word began to spread about the museum. Of course, not everyone was supportive. I heard not only from the white lawyer, but from a black professor from Fort Valley State College, who called to tell me a black-oriented museum was none of my business. I was undaunted. "This is a project that should have been started long before me but wasn't, for whatever reasons, and I'm moving forward," I told him. "Positive ideas are welcomed."

Another person said I would have been better off trying to get a small basement room in the Museum of Arts and Sciences in north Macon. One friend feared that I might be killed for opening an African-American museum and was, quite sweetly, sincerely concerned.

As we began the work of transforming the building into a museum, I never received any threats, nor did I worry. One or two times, I wondered if someone might deface the place. But I put that concern aside, and it never occurred. The people of Macon watched mostly with curiosity.

Once the building was cleaned out, we decided to hold a reception to show it off. We invited Bishop Joseph Francis from Newark, New Jersey, to bless the museum. Bishop Francis was a very engaging, forward-thinking bishop. Earlier, when I was raising money for the project, I had asked our local bishop to help us try to tap into a national fund available through the Church. He declined to do so. His lack of support, when so many others could see the museum's potential, was disappointing.

Because it rained, the blessing of the museum was actually held at Stewart Chapel, an A.M.E. church. Afterward, we moved the reception to the museum, with White Brothers Auto Parts store next door providing the lights.

The museum opened in 1985, four years after I purchased the building. During the first three years, we continued the remodeling. Harry and Mary Durham stuccoed and reshaped the entire outside of the building, making it presentable. Albert became the contractor for the renovations and, as a county commissioner, kept us abreast of political matters. Dr. D.T. Walton and others gave financial support. Many professors from Fort Valley State came to our aid, lending their professional expertise.

At one point, we held a fundraising event at the Sidney Lanier Cottage, birthplace of the celebrated Confederate poet. It was ironic that we, from the Harriet Tubman African-American Museum, were using his home to raise money. We had a wonderful turnout with many distinguished people from both the black and white communities.

Downtown since has become the home of other museums, bringing new life and tourism to our beautiful city. I feel that the Tubman led this revival and helps every day to bolster the local arts community. The Tubman also continues to help promote racial understanding.

The museum is on track to move to a new, much bigger home on Cherry Street in the spring of 2015. Though I'm not involved in the day-to-day operation of the Tubman, I couldn't be more proud.

The museum's director hopes it can be an anchor for downtown. In addition to the exhibits, and the educational programs that will be offered there, the museum will host reunions, weddings and other happy family gatherings.

Often, I visit the current museum to say hello to the staff, and I am sometimes welcomed by a couple of hundred school children and their teachers. To see children there, looking over the exhibits, always makes me leave with a smile on my face. Their presence is all the validation I will ever need.

CHAPTER 30

HER HOUSE WAS BUILT A few yards off Walnut Street in Pleasant Hill, Macon's first black neighborhood. Started in the late 1800s, Pleasant Hill was originally populated by the city's African-American doctors, teachers, ministers and businessmen. It was a thriving area made up of L-shaped Victorian cottages, corner stores and St. Peter Claver Catholic Church.

In the early 1960s, the government cut a swath through the neighborhood to make room for Interstate 75. More than 100 houses and two churches were demolished. Many people left the neighborhood, which began to quickly deteriorate. But Willie P. Thomas stayed.

Willie lived in a small, brown frame house several feet lower than the street, so there were a few steps leading down to her front door. Her car was parked in a metal shelter. The front door had four flimsy panes of glass. It would have been easy for any intruder to get into the house. But, even after the neighborhood became drug infested, no one dared to trespass.

Willie was in her 70s when we first met. She had become a Catholic when she was a little girl going to St. Peter Claver School, run by the Sisters of the Blessed Sacrament. She met Mother Katharine Drexel, the Philadelphia heiress who began the religious order and financed the building of Macon's St. Peter Claver School and dozens of others around the country to educate African Americans and Native Americans.

I often visited Willie and her brother, Bud, who came to live with her in his later years. He would be lying on a simple metal cot in the front room. Bud had been the janitor at St. Joseph's Catholic Church for maybe 30 or 40 years. He was living out his old age with no retirement money. Willie loved him dearly.

In his room, there was one metal folding chair and an old chifforobe containing his clothes. Next to Bud's cot was a small table with a lamp and a pile of old papers. An open gas space heater warmed the place in the winter, and a floor fan feebly battled Macon's 90- to 100-degree summers.

Pictures, letters, prayers and cards were tacked up or hung up all over. These were Willie's treasures from countless friends. When you walked into the house, a room was to the right, its door always closed. In Willie's room, she kept a piece of a bed made from a single cot with a mattress on top, a TV that sometimes worked with rabbit ears, a floor heater, and an old window unit air conditioner, precariously plugged into an extension cord. One lone 75-watt light bulb hung from the ceiling, casting harsh, direct light. Willie's wheelchair was usually parked nearby. If invited to stay, a visitor would go back to Bud's room to get the metal folding chair.

The tiny kitchen held a 24-year-old refrigerator, an old sink and minimal shelf and workspace. Another refrigerator that was even older sat on a small screened porch.

Gallon plastic jugs lined the back porch. They were used to hold water from nearby Indian Springs.

Many new parishioners at St. Peter Claver Church would immediately fall in love with Willie, called Bill by some and Reverend by a few others. She was friendly, intelligent and strong. Sometimes people would visit Willie's home and then come to me, asking if they could leave a donation for her. Sometimes, they suggested that church members get together and go over to Willie's home and fix the outside, clean inside and help her financially. I would smile and assure them that Willie did not need our help. I knew she could do what she wanted to do, financially. She chose to live modestly.

Willie told me many stories during our visits.

"When I graduated from high school, they needed black teachers. I began to teach school right away and to go to Fort Valley College. In the summer time, I would work for white families and take care of their children. I loved it. They would take me to the ocean beaches with their families, and all I would have to do would be cook and take care of the children part of the day. I would have a lot of the day and most of the evenings to do what I wanted. This way, I was able to travel a lot, see many places and meet many interesting people. I never felt like a servant, only a helper.

"My daddy and momma always taught me that I was as good as anyone else. He was a cobbler in Macon. But, when my mother got sick, the doctor told him to move to the country because it would be better for her health. He up and bought 167 acres of land in Monroe County, and we moved to the country on a farm. He loved momma very much.

"When I graduated from Fort Valley, I got what we called a real job, not as a maid, but with the Board of Education. We were paid $33 per month, and the white teachers were paid $100 per month. That's why I've been so blessed since retirement."

I asked, "How is that?"

"The law now says that everyone is to be paid the same, and I get the same retirement as white teachers. I got my master's from New York City College and my six-year degree at Columbia University. We were not allowed to go to the University of Georgia, but the State of Georgia paid our way to go to graduate school up north. Now I get paid as a master's degree holder with about 50 years of teaching. I never had so much money."

Willie had a mastectomy in her 70s. She became arthritic and always struggled, but continued to push herself. Even in her 80s and early 90s, she would take her cane and hobble out to her carport. She would get in her old Buick and drive to the Kroger on the posh north side of Macon. "They have better produce than the local stores in our neighborhood," she would say.

She refused help from anyone. Willie would get to the parking lot of the store and tug at the wheelchair in the back seat of her car until she got it out. As she shopped, she would use the wheelchair was a walker. She would place the groceries in the seat of the chair, walk back to the car and put the groceries in the back seat. Then she would struggle to fold the chair and push it back into the car. She would head home and somehow get her groceries into the house using her walking cane to maneuver the steps.

When Willie and I first met, she headed the church's Brownie and Girl Scouts troops. It was great the way these little girls would flock around this elderly woman. Later on, she formed a club for elderly women, and she was also the leader of it. The women would call her "Reverend" because she was the person in charge everywhere she went. She was a moral and religious leader who encouraged and listened to others. She was never bossy. But, if need be, she would tell others what was best.

"Willie, how are you doing?" I asked her one day.

"I ain't much, but I'm bumping," she said.

"You look good to me. I wish I had your energy, and I hope I do as well when I get to your age."

"But Father," said Willie, then 93, "it takes me so long to get out of bed and to get my clothes on. I don't even feel like getting dressed some days."

I began to commiserate with her and said something to the effect, "I'm not as fast as I used to be either."

Willie looked up at me smiling and said, "That's right. You aren't as fast as you used to be, and you aren't as slow as you're going to be."

I teased her. "Willie, someday, I'm going to be able to outwit you."

I have never forgotten the lessons she taught me, zest for life, how to grow old, how to love people, how to live simply.

Willie was aware of racism in society and in the Church, but it never seemed to upset her. She would state her case clearly, but she would not get bent out of shape. She had lived through much and remembered well the days when even an old catechism of the Diocese of Savannah talked about the inferiority of black people.

My mother visited me in Macon before she became sick, and she and Willie became friends. After my mother went into a nursing home, Willie would send her birthday and Christmas cards until my mother died in 1994 at the age of 94.

When Willie was on her deathbed, in 1995 at the age of 95, I visited her every day. By then, Bud was dead. He had heart disease and had suffered a stroke before going into a mediocre nursing home, where he lived a few months. Her brother's experience helped Willie make up her mind she wanted to die at home.

She consented to hiring some help to look after her, but only under the condition that the person would never call for an ambulance that would take her to a hospital or nursing home.

After she died, lovely and expensive antique furniture was found in the room she had shut off. And, to the amazement of many, the little old lady in the run-down house left thousands of dollars to St. Peter Claver Church and to the Tubman Museum.

CHAPTER 31

BOBBY JONES WAS BORN IN Chicago and raised in Macon's Tindall Heights, in the shadow of Mercer University.

Campus police kicked his butt several times when he was a boy because he and his friends were often caught roaming the school grounds, despite warnings to stay away. As a man, he would become the first African-American professor awarded tenure there.

Many people owe Bobby a debt of gratitude, including me. He always seemed larger than life, the way he effortlessly put people at ease and smoothed over conflict.

He was one of my best friends, and I often took my troubles to him. He was a straight shooter who would tell you what you needed to hear, not so much what you wanted to hear.

We met when I was 42, and he was 43. He was president of St. Peter Claver's parish council. When I attended my first meeting, shortly after moving to Macon, I didn't know exactly what a parish council did. None of my previous parishes had one. The Trinitarian order decided how money would be spent.

"That's Dr. Bobby Jones, a professor of education at Mercer," someone pointed out with great pride.

He was tall, 6 feet 4 inches, and handsome, with a ready smile. We walked toward each other, extending our hands and introducing ourselves. "It's nice to meet you, and I hope you enjoy your days at St. Peter Claver," he said.

"Thanks, Dr. Jones," I said. "I'm happy to be here, and it's a pleasure to meet you. I understand that you are the president of the parish council. I can surely use your help."

"Father, please, call me Bobby," he replied.

"Glad to, Bobby," I said, smiling.

Bobby was good at running the meetings. He invited feedback, but kept people on subject. He cut off excessive discussion in the interest of time, but never came across as rude.

I watched the parish council proceedings with interest. Then I noticed something. I didn't know if parish councils worked the same everywhere, but it seemed members of St. Peter Claver's council spent a lot of time deciding what the pastor should do. Right away, I could see this could be a problem.

Sure, I wanted the council to make suggestions for projects to pursue, but I also felt I had enough ideas and creative energy to think of my own.

The council came up with several assignments for me during that first meeting. I asked Bobby if I could address the members. I wanted to make sure they knew that this was not what I envisioned.

"I'm happy that you vote on the things you want done in the parish, and you've voted on some very good projects," I said. "But I'm going to have to ask for your help. I have more than enough to do. You should go ahead with these projects and be the leaders and doers. I will support you."

I told them I was interested in a more collaborative relationship and shared some of my ideas. Though I said these words nicely, I couldn't tell if council members had taken them the right way.

The meeting ended, and refreshments were served. I anxiously awaited their feedback, but no one really brought up what I had said. When everyone left, I walked the few steps back to the rectory.

Worried that I had come across as dismissive of their ideas, I decided to call Bobby that night.

"Bobby, this is Father Keil, I know it's late and we just had the meeting, but may I see you tomorrow or the next day for a few minutes?"

"Sure, Father," he said. "What are you doing for breakfast? Could we meet at Shoney's?"

"That would be great. Thanks so much," I answered.

The next morning, I was still quite anxious about what kind of first impression I had made. I headed to the restaurant, eager to clear up any misunderstandings. The last thing I wanted was for him and the others to think that I was trying to change the way the parish operated before I had even had a chance to see it.

Bobby was already there.

"Hi, Father," he said cheerfully.

"Hey, Bobby. How are you doing so early in the morning? Thanks for coming," I said.

"Glad to, Father. I have an early class to teach anyway, so it's no problem."

We got seated, ordered our breakfast and began to talk. "Bobby, I felt badly last night when I told the parish council that they may vote on anything they wish, but I have enough to do." I told him I had brought up some of my ideas for the parish so that council members would know where my head was, not because I wasn't interested in their input.

Bobby smiled and, without batting an eye, said, "Father, it was the best meeting we've had in the years I've been at St. Peter Claver Church." He said he was happy to hear my ideas.

"You put your agenda on the table, and you told us to be upfront," he said. "You said that you were not stopping us from deliberating and voting and choosing projects as a parish council. What more can we expect? I think the meeting went wonderfully, and I am happy with how it turned out. I talked with other members, and they were also happy."

I hardly believed what I was hearing. I had rarely been so pleasantly surprised.

It was the first of many meetings at the Shoney's, both to deal with parish issues and later just to grab lunch as buddies. I respected Bobby's opinions. He and his wife became beloved friends. I would go to their house after Christmas Mass or sometimes accompany them to other holiday gatherings.

I buried his mother. I also buried his brother. Bobby told me why he asked me to preside over their funerals. "My relatives do not go to a church, and I know that you will be respectful to them and not castigate the family. The stupid practice some preachers have of trying to put a guilt trip on families at the funeral is still around.

"Some preachers worry about membership, which translates into revenue and bigger collections and, they hope, a bigger, richer church. They talk about a heaven they have never seen and know nothing about. The only thing they know about heaven and hell is what they have heard or read from other preachers who know nothing about heaven or hell."

I felt his anger over how judgmental and falsely pious some in the clergy were. I was happy he didn't include me.

Over the years, Bobby introduced me to many people in Macon's African-American community. He was active in Macon's Morehouse Alumni group. With him introducing me, many of the barriers that often exist between black and white men broke down quite readily.

He was a man with great leadership skills. Mercer University made use of these skills, often asking Bobby to head accreditation processes. He frequently was chosen to moderate large meetings for community groups because of his ability to be fair, coolheaded and efficient. He used intelligence to deal with prejudice and ignorance, which he had encountered many times in life, always rising above.

Georgia colleges were still segregated when Bobby decided to go. He attended historically black Morehouse College and, during the summers, picked cotton for spending money. He wanted to go to graduate school, but couldn't in Georgia. The state had a policy of paying for black students to attend colleges up north, instead of integrating, thereby keeping Georgia universities lily white. Georgia's backwardness allowed Bobby to attend the Ivy League's Columbia University, just as Willie Thomas did before him.

After graduate school, he became a teacher. He held the job as the first African-American principal over an integrated school in Macon – for a little while. The school superintendent offered him the job and asked if he had any requests. Bobby stated that he had two requests. One was that any teacher, black or white, be free to transfer out of the school before he came. The second request was that the classrooms be painted. He wanted students to know – if only from looking at a fresh, well-kept building – that the administration cared about them.

August came, and Bobby went to the school on the appointed day and found none of the classrooms painted. Bobby called the superintendent, who asked him to come to the school board's office. The superintendent was upset. "Goddamn, I just put $50,000 into new toilet seats in the black schools. The whites sure as hell can't use those old toilet seats that blacks used. I will paint when I get damn ready."

Bobby struggled with the decision of whether he should go back to the school. He talked it over with his wife that night. He had recently received an invitation to teach at Mercer University and had planned to turn down that opportunity to take the principal position. But he knew he couldn't work for that superintendent, so he called him, refused the job and went to work for Mercer University. At Mercer, his stature only grew.

When I was starting the Tubman Museum, I depended on Bobby's steady judgment. And he often sought my advice on issues. When he was turned down for a promotion at Mercer, we spent untold hours talking about his pain and whether he truly fit in there.

He called me and asked me to come to his home one day. He had been struggling with illness.

"Father, I'm going to die," he said.

We talked for a long time. After a couple of hours, I left saying, "I love you and your family, and they love you much."

I visited him while he was in the hospital, and he went down fast. Though he's been dead for many years now, I still tell people about him and pray for him to this very day.

Bobby once told me a great story about education. "When I was a little boy in second grade, the teacher put children into groups," he said. "The groups were seemingly based on intelligence and behavior. I was in the lowest group, the black birds. The teacher always pointed out to visitors who the black birds were and talked negatively about them. Then she bragged about the yellow or red birds. Whenever a visitor came into our room, I put my head down and tried to hide. I did poorly in school and felt stupid.

"The next year, I went to a new class. The teacher announced that there were no black birds, red birds, yellow birds, or any other birds. She told us repeatedly, 'You can and you will.' All of a sudden my grades took off, and I was getting an A in all of my classes. Father, that teacher taught me about learning and teaching, and she changed my life. She said, 'You can, and you will.' "

Well, Bobby Jones could, and he did. I have rarely met another with all of his gifts, goodness and strength.

CHAPTER 32

I HAD BEEN EXPECTING IT for a while.

Thirteen years is a long time for a diocesan priest to spend in one location. So, in late 1987, when the Bishop and I discussed the possibility of me moving to Savannah, I did not protest. I felt good about my accomplishments in Macon and, in many ways, welcomed a new challenge.

St. Peter Claver was thriving. Church membership was increasing. The number of baptisms was up. We had completed a renovation of the school, and its endowment stood at $1 million. The church had secured the land next door to build a new rectory. On a personal level, I had developed strong relationships with congregation members, as well as ministers at Macon's other churches and synagogues. I had managed to complete doctoral course work at Emory's Candler School of Theology. The Tubman Museum was stable and in good hands.

The Bishop and I mutually agreed that I would go to Savannah and begin my work at St. Mary in February 1988. It was not easy to tell St. Peter Claver's congregation that I would be leaving. Some members sent a petition to the Bishop, asking that he reconsider the transfer. He declined, and I left Macon feeling hopeful, and at ease, about my next assignment.

St. Mary was a mostly poor church, with a majority black congregation.

Because of its set-up, it was difficult to manage. The church and the rectory were located on one block, and the school, which the diocese had closed, was on another. No fence separated the school building and playground from the declining neighborhood, so the property attracted vagrants and vandalism. Upkeep was almost a full-time job. Because the church didn't have a reception hall, a couple of the classrooms in the school were used once or twice a week. That meant church members had to walk the sometimes dangerous streets. And it meant the parish had to pay to keep the building air-conditioned, heated and cleaned.

Church members, many of whom were looking for new energy in their parish, warmly welcomed me to Savannah. The Bishop welcomed me, too, for a while.

I spent my first weeks there talking to parishioners about their frustrations. Many felt forgotten by the diocese and overwhelmed by church's property maintenance issues. I came up with a plan to address their concerns: first, unburden the parish by selling the school. Then build a small facility for receptions and classes near the church and rectory, thereby consolidating the property. That would allow us to get on with the real work of revitalizing the parish and coming up with projects aimed at improving the neighborhood.

I met with the Bishop on my birthday and was surprised when he rejected my ideas without offering suggestions on what we should do instead. He recognized the problems we had, but still wanted to maintain the status quo. I couldn't understand his decision or his anger when I defended the rationale for my plan.

He couldn't understand why I was questioning him. He brought up a number of other occasions, during my time in Macon, when I had challenged his decisions. He wanted to make sure I understood he had the authority to make these decisions and didn't need to explain himself to me. When he questioned my mental stability – basically because we didn't see eye-to-eye – it was the last straw.

I had been growing more and more disillusioned with the Catholic Church. It was becoming harder for me to deal with the harsh way the Church sometimes treated its members.

The Church's hierarchy seemed to want to shut down all debate on important issues. Take the unfair way women were treated. Many were asking the valid question, if women can be baptized, why can't they be ordained? But their question was falling on deaf ears. Over the course of my life, I had met many women who would have made outstanding priests. It was wrong to let tradition be a barrier.

Some people couldn't understand why I would question the Church on such matters. But the Church is not perfect, every teaching is not infallible, and disagreement is allowed. That's why God gave each of us a conscience.

And my conscience was also struggling with the way the Church was handling a growing pedophilia scandal. For years, the Church refused to recognize that it had a problem, even as scores of complaints poured in in the 1970s and 1980s about priests sexually abusing children.

I remember discussing these and other issues with another priest, and he said outright, "If I had $10,000, I would leave the priesthood."

That conversation made me think long and hard about what it would take for me to leave. So much of my identity and sense of self-worth seemed tied to being a priest. The wonderful people I had met during my ministry – Thelma, Paul Anthony, Esau, Sister Renee, Willie, to name a few – had shaped me into the person I was. But I asked myself if I was still in a situation where I could learn and grow.

After my meeting with the Bishop, I knew I was not.

I couldn't see myself acting as just a property manager for an intown church. And the Bishop's decision to shut down our conversation signaled to me that he had given up on the possibility of a vibrant black Catholic ministry in Savannah.

Studying to be a Trinitarian had been hard for me. The priests micro-managed every aspect of a seminarian's life. A number of them drank too much. Some were polite racists. Throughout that time, I grappled with anxiety and depression. But I stayed focused on the day I would be a priest, out serving people's spiritual and physical needs.

I had been lucky at Holy Trinity and St. Peter Claver. For the most part, I was allowed to decide, along with church members, what was best for our parishes. It was clear to me that it would be different in Savannah, in the Bishop's back yard, and I knew I couldn't go back to being treated like a child. It was a lost cause.

There's no graceful way to leave the priesthood. But, in the wee hours following my conversation with the Bishop, I decided it was time.

CHAPTER 33

YOU'RE SUPPOSED TO BE A priest forever. In good times and in bad. In sickness and in health.

That thinking is pounded into every priest's DNA, and it is not easy to overcome. But, with much prayer, meditation and help from my friends, I started the healing process. The mobile home and four acres I had bought in Twiggs County were my refuge. It was a peaceful spot, with plenty of trees, the perfect place to think about my past and future.

But I had no intention of taking up a hermit's life. I rented office space on busy Riverside Drive in Macon and put up a sign for counseling services. Because I had so many connections in the city, clients started coming right away. Star Choices, an excellent organization that provides homes and community-based services for people with developmental disabilities, offered me work in staff development. Different companies also hired me and Rosalind McMillan to occasionally lead seminars on racial tolerance and understanding. For a very brief period, I even worked at the Tubman Museum, but I felt so guilty drawing a paycheck that I had to quit.

Some friends offered money to help get me started in my new life. Thankfully, while money was a concern, it wasn't a pressing issue. I had always been a saver, but especially after meeting Father Galvin.

Father Galvin was a very faithful and dedicated priest. In terms of his personality, I count myself lucky if I share any of his marvelous attributes. But I was also afraid of becoming Father Galvin. He lived out his later years penniless. He often had to ask people for lunch money. His clothes were threadbare.

I had seen many older priests in his situation, worried about retirement and how they would make it. It's not as though the Church didn't have enough resources to make sure they didn't spend their older years that way. The Church just allowed it to happen. I promised myself that I would not be that poor when I was 70.

I never had much money, but I had learned from a broker friend in Columbus, Georgia, that, from time to time, I should invest $50 to $100 in stocks. I began to do this and was happy to see how my little money grew, even in the 1970s, which were bad years for investing. The money I had socked away kept me from panicking when I was forced to reinvent myself at 55.

Of course, leaving the priesthood – or any other lifelong endeavor – is not simply an issue of money. It's also about finding your confidence again. Before you can reinvent yourself, they say, you have to know who you are. You can't expand yourself by doing same things you've always done. I tried to honestly assess my strengths and weaknesses.

My work as a counselor was fulfilling but paid a meager salary. I kept my eyes open for other opportunities. Pat Cramer, a beloved friend who had been a St. Peter Claver parishioner, suggested that I might do well in the brokerage business. I had considered this before. With Pat's encouragement, I decided to actively pursue such a job.

Driving around one day, I noticed a small brokerage firm near my counseling office. I decided to ask the people there what the industry was really like and for advice about getting started.

I first met with Raymond Smith Jr., the son of the owner of the firm.

The interview was congenial, and we made another appointment for me to meet with his parents. In my interview with Raymond Smith Sr. and his wife, Kathleen, I listened carefully as they talked about the business. Mutual friends had told them I was a good person, so they had pretty much already made up their minds to hire me.

I asked for no draw — only commissions. My other jobs would give me money to live on while I learned the investment business. I worked hard, studied, learned from others. The Smiths were very supportive and never pressured me to produce. The first year, I made only $7,500. In the next several years, my income well exceeded my expectations.

Outside of work, I tried to stay busy. I exercised. Friends invited me to dinner. They talked me through moments of self-doubt.

I knew when I came back to Macon I would face questions from parishioners and others about why I had left the priesthood. Of course, many of my close friends knew. Talking to everyone else, I kept my answers short but honest and avoided bad-mouthing the Church. By and large, people were very kind. There were a few who simply couldn't understand my decision and no longer wanted to be a part of my life. I respected their position and moved on. What else could I do?

The priests in town – Father Liam Collins, who had taken over at St. Peter Claver, along with Father Bob Cushing from Holy Spirit, and others – were nothing but supportive.

Once, I went to Mass at St. Peter Claver and was incredibly moved when parishioners gave me a standing ovation. But I never went back. I didn't want to become a distraction.

I continued to pray and meditate on my own. A Baptist preacher in town offered to ordain me so I could carry on my ministry. I was grateful but declined.

As always, nuns provided a source of strength and encouragement. I maintained strong ties with sisters at St. Peter Claver and elsewhere. As author Anna Quindlen once said, "If there is anyone who's living the work of the New Testament, it's the nuns of the Catholic church and not the Catholic hierarchy." So many times in my life, I found this to be true. These strong, dedicated, insightful women offered me advice and friendship. I talked with them often as I transitioned into my new life.

CHAPTER 34

BEFORE THE CANCER, SHE HAD been a tall, vibrant and elegant black woman. But, as she lay in a hospital bed in Jackson, Mississippi, Sister Thea Bowman looked tired and thin. She smiled at me, but was clearly in pain. I knew this likely would be our last visit.

Nurses, aides and doctors walked in and out on the polished green floors. On the adjustable tray table next to her, Thea's leftover supper of mixed vegetables and roast beef gave off an unappetizing odor. Get-well cards from people all over the United States hung on the pale green walls, and flowers lined the windowsill and tables. Every few minutes, a doctor was paged over the loudspeaker.

Perhaps some of the hospital staff had heard of Sister Thea. After entering the convent at 15, the little girl from the little Mississippi town of Canton had become a national figure, at least in Catholic circles. She helped introduce black

American culture and song into the Catholic liturgy and was a key figure in the founding of the Institute of Black Catholic Studies at Xavier University in New Orleans. She was a poet, evangelist and singer who performed classical music recitals and organized revivals from San Francisco to New York, from Macon to Minneapolis. Now she was alone and dying.

She began to wince with pain and cry out. I wiped the tears from her face and quietly cried myself.

"The Lord has been so good to me, and many people have been good to me," she said. "Beloved Sister Evelyn lives with me and looks after me. I lack nothing. I have so many friends. I just don't want to die because there is so much I want to do! But, God's will be done, and I do accept it."

I had first heard of Sister Thea in the early 1960s. The Trinitarians had a mission church and school in Canton. Priests and others spoke of this fantastically talented person who had gone to their church and school, then went gone off to Wisconsin to become a nun.

I did not meet her until I invited her to come and give a weekend of talks at Holy Trinity. We had long conversations that weekend and I asked for her feedback on what we were doing there. We also talked about her life and some of the struggles she was facing. After that, we remained friends over the years. She came to Macon to speak at St. Peter Claver and stood by me through my decision to leave the priesthood. When it seemed clear that she was dying, she called me in 1990 to tell me the news. I knew I had to see her.

"Richard, you drove so far!" Sister Thea said from her hospital bed. "How are you? I have treasured your letters, our talks and the times with you giving retreats at your churches."

I took her hand. "Thea, thanks for your words. We have known each other a long time, since I was studying for the priesthood with the Trinitarians and heard them talking about you. I wondered who you were. They seemed to hold you in great awe."

Thea laughed. "Yes, some of them are great priests and some of them are part of the problems we have. Many people know me and think they understand me. They also think they understand the issues of black people. There is a large space between meeting someone and understanding the issues."

Thea looked at me. "Richard, how much time do you have? You and I know that I am dying, and I don't want to die bitter about anything. There are some things I would like to resolve in my heart. Can you stay and talk with me?"

I smiled and replied, "Thea, I have as long as you wish. Tell me when you get tired, and I'll leave. Just let me know."

I felt honored that this spiritual and intellectual giant thought talking to me, though I no longer wore a collar, might provide any comfort. For many years before I left the priesthood, she had shared her spiritual journey with me and kept me up-to-date with what was happening nationally in the Church.

"Richard, I am tired. Even my hair is graying. Lordy, I have seen so much! The Church has been good to me, and it has been cruel at times to my brothers and sisters. There were great priests here in Mississippi like Father Luke, who was well loved by the black community. His house was under armed guard in the 1960s and Martin Luther King would use his church, school and gym as rest stops for the marchers as they came through. Father Luke did it because he was willing to live or die for us. Now we get priests who are either afraid of us or just don't care to know us. Sometimes, they have serious personal problems and can't help anyone. They haven't hurt me personally, but they hurt the community, and that hurts me."

Sister Thea knew there were good priests out there who felt crippled and disaffected. She knew that there were priests, like me, making the decision to leave.

"Sometimes, when I've traveled across the nation, I've seen many good clergy in pain because of celibacy issues. Some have relationships with women or get into alcohol or other bad situations. Some were gay and struggled with how to handle it. I have talked with bishops about this, but many just keep a hard line. Some are very sympathetic, but they tell me they have no power to change anything. Some bishops have serious problems themselves. God, Richard, why can't something be changed? Why can't the church be more open? Why does justice seem to come only with a struggle? I guess this is why I am so tired and worn out."

Thea would be leaving this world, but knew there were so many issues to be addressed.

I listened as she continued to talk, and my heart ached for many reasons. I was angry because she was young, 53, and dying of cancer. I was frustrated that she had spent so much time frustrated in her life, knowing that the church wanted to attract more black people, but then abused them by turning a blind eye to their struggles. Sisters, in general, were not treated well. Black nuns were treated even worse. It pissed me off.

"Sister, I have never thought that you were eaten up with bitterness, and I know you have been welcoming and loving to your white brothers and sisters. People from all over love you, and the reason they do is not because you have a Ph.D. or sing so beautifully. It is because you are not afraid to cross the line that separates people. You cross the line and invite others to cross the line with you. You are flat-out wonderful."

I was crying, and Sister was crying. She put her hand out and I held it.

"Let's pray, Thea. God has given us the opportunity to know one another for many years. Now our paths cross again."

I began, "Lord, thank you for this dear woman who has shown so many people how to love and how to live. She has been on a long journey, loving, singing, teaching and praying from one end of our country to the other. She walked the roads to the poorest cabins in Mississippi. She spent countless hours with the smallest of children. She has been patient with people and taught thousands of sisters, priests and bishops how to address issues of racial justice. She has given pride to her religious order, made her hometown aware of the world, and made the world aware of her hometown. She has loved and been faithful to you, Lord. Thank you for sending her into my life and for sharing so many of her gifts with me. Bless Thea now and give her strength and peace."

Thea looked up. "Thanks, Keil. I love and appreciate you."

I began to leave and told her I would always remember her in my prayers. "Love you much, and God bless."

We were both crying. I kissed her hand and said, "Good night, Thea."

"Good night, and God bless, Richard."

CHAPTER 35

I INSTANTLY RECOGNIZED THE VOICE on the other end of the line. Charlie Liteky had been a friend for 40 years. At one time, we had been seminarians together, back when I was Emil and he was called Angelo. Now we were both former priests.

"Charlie!" I exclaimed. "It's wonderful to hear from you. How are you and Judy and your brother Pat?"

"I'm fine," he said. "Judy, Pat and I are here for the sentencing at 1:30 p.m." He said it casually, as though it was perfectly normal to be awaiting a prison sentence. And, frankly, for him and his brother, it wasn't unusual.

"Who is to be sentenced?" I asked.

In the days of old, I would have followed his case in the newspaper, at the very least. These days, between working as a counselor and financial adviser, I had time to give the newspaper only a superficial read. Still I knew this involved some kind of peace protest.

Charlie and his brother had been involved in many such protests in past years. This time, the two had been working with Father Roy Bourgeois and others to persuade Congress to close the School of Americas located at Fort Benning. The school trained military groups from Latin America in low intensity warfare. Many of its graduates have gone back home to commit atrocious human rights abuses, such as the November 1989 murders of six Jesuit priests, their housekeeper and her daughter at Central American University in El Salvador.

Father Bourgeois formed the School of the Americas Watch in 1990 to protest the school. The Litekys had always been among his staunchest supporters.

"Emil, I mean Richard, I am to be sentenced, along with Sister Marie," Charlie responded.

I worried often about Charlie and Pat. They had truly sacrificed and suffered for the poor in the name of peace and nonviolence. "Are you OK?" I asked.

Charlie laughed, saying, "Dick, I'm fine. We all are fine. I just wanted to call you and talk with you because you have always meant a lot to me. Pat wants to talk to you, too, so please call him in room 241 here at the motel."

His laugh was genuine, and his spirits were good. "The attorney for the government is one of the best lawyers I have ever known," he continued. "I think the judge is a good man."

Charlie and Pat were remarkable men. They were never hostile toward the people who convicted, fined and sentenced them to federal prison for their nonviolent protests, even though the price of their prosecution and confinement was steep. It meant time away from family and friends, and estrangement from those who couldn't understand how men of God could break the law.

Some years back, Charlie and his wife had thought about divorcing to try to limit the impact his protesting could have on her. "It wasn't because we didn't love one another," Charlie said. "I thought that the government would take our home from us. If we divorced, I wouldn't have to worry about her being hurt. Thankfully, nothing like that has happened, so we are still married. But it is hard for her when I'm in jail."

Charlie and I talked for a few more minutes before I had to hang up. I thanked him for calling and assured him that I would be praying for him. I also told him I admired him. "I don't have your courage. You are a beloved person. God bless."

"Please call Pat," Charlie reminded me. "He wants to speak to you." I promised that I would and jotted down the number of the motel.

I finished up my appointments for the day and went home. But I couldn't get Charlie's phone call out of my mind. Memories of the two of them – and their brother Jim – kept popping into my head.

I had attended their father's burial at Arlington National Cemetery and their mother's funeral in Jacksonville, Florida.

Their dad had been an officer on an aircraft carrier during WWII. He was a pilot and would aggravate his wife when they were stationed in Hawaii by buzzing their home. One day on the carrier, a cable snapped and hit him. He was crippled for the rest of his life, confined to his bed. He made the best of it, recording jokes, stories and words of encouragement to others in similar situations.

All of his boys were strong, tall and good looking. Charlie and Jim played football and basketball. Charlie decided to study for the priesthood with the Trinitarians. He was an immediate star in the seminary because he was such a good athlete, had a marvelous singing voice, wonderful people skills and a good mind.

Just as I was, he was assigned to work in the inner city of Washington, D.C., as a seminarian. The people there loved him, and he loved the people. The time was the late '50s and early '60s. He taught me a lot about dealing with people – adults and children. He never had to yell at the children to get their attention during the day camp activities. He would just raise one hand and begin to look at his wristwatch. All the children knew Charlie's rule. He was counting the seconds it took them to quiet down. The longer it took, the less time they would have in the next fun activity. If it took 30 seconds to quiet down, he would take 30 seconds away from playtime. I always thought it was a great way to get the attention of children and avoid yelling all day.

Charlie thrived in his role. However, when he got back to the seminary in late summer, he would be called The Big Nigger because of his good relationship with African Americans. I had often heard priests working in the black community called nigger priests.

When Charlie was ordained, he was assigned to work in a retreat center in New Jersey. Again, he was very popular among parishioners. The other priests, brothers and sisters were jealous. This greatly affected Charlie. He asked for permission to see a psychiatrist, but the custodian general refused.

Father Leonard, a priest in Virginia, asked the custodian general if Charlie could be his assistant, and permission was granted. It was a good solution for everyone. Father Leonard welcomed Charlie's gifts.

At the time, the Vietnam War was in full swing. You either supported it or you were against it. Family members often were at odds. Charlie received permission to become a Catholic chaplain in the Army, a position that was in great need. He went to Vietnam and, not surprisingly, became a hero. He received our country's highest military award – the Medal of Honor – at a special White House ceremony.

The citation says that Charlie – serving with Company A, 4th Battalion, 12th Infantry, 199th Light Infantry Brigade – was participating in a search and destroy operation when Company A came under intense fire from a battalion size enemy force.

"Observing two wounded men, Chaplain Liteky moved to within 15 meters of an enemy machine gun position to reach them, placing himself between the enemy and the wounded men. When there was a brief respite in the fighting, he managed to drag them to the relative safety of the landing zone. Inspired by his courageous actions, the company rallied and began placing a heavy volume of fire upon the enemy's positions. In a magnificent display of courage and leadership, Chaplain Liteky began moving upright through the enemy fire, administering last rites to the dying and evacuating the wounded. Noticing another trapped and seriously wounded man, Chaplain Liteky crawled to his aid. Realizing that the wounded man was too heavy to carry, he rolled on his back, placed the man on his chest and, through sheer determination and fortitude crawled back to the landing zone using his elbows and heels to push himself along."

Charlie wasn't done. According to the citation, he paused to catch his breath, then "returned to the action and came upon a man entangled in the dense, thorny underbrush. Once more, intense enemy fire was directed at him, but Chaplain Liteky stood his ground and calmly broke the vines and carried the man to the landing zone for evacuation. On several occasions when the landing zone was under small arms and rocket fire, Chaplain Liteky stood up in the face of hostile fire and personally directed the medevac helicopters into and out of the area."

Charlie carried more than 20 men to the landing zone for evacuation. Later, it was discovered that he had wounds in the neck and foot.

Charlie went to Vietnam three times, and each time was stationed in a combat zone. He wanted to be with the men on the front.

Some wanted to make Charlie the poster boy of the great brave chaplain. Here was a man who founded and heavily funded an orphanage in Vietnam. Those in the peace movement wanted him to come out against the war. Charlie was torn. He thought long and hard.

Ultimately, he decided to leave the priesthood. He wanted to spend his time speaking up for peace and nonviolence. In the mid-1980s, he renounced his Congressional Medal of Honor. He's also given up the monthly stipend the United States government sends to all recipients of this very precious medal.

Even today, Charlie carries physical and mental scars from Vietnam. Still, he's manages to stay strong. Somehow, Charlie found the strength to go find the body of his brother Jim when he died in a diving accident. Jim played college basketball and had just begun a singing career. He had an adventurous spirit and liked to go cave diving.

During one of those excursions, he drowned. The Navy Seals looked for him, but were unable to locate his body. Charlie was allowed to go to the scene, where he found his brother.

I don't agree with all that Charlie does, but I do profoundly respect his courage and character. Judges and prosecutors lecture him, calling him self-righteous. Maybe. But he's earned the right.

Pat was dedicated to the peace movement, as well.

The next day after talking to Charlie, I called Pat. I asked him about the sentencing.

"Richard, I'm surprised that Charlie got one whole year and a $10,000 fine," he said. "That's so hard on the part of the judge. There was a U.S. Marshal standing near me all during the trial because they probably thought I was going to do something. Sister got six months."

"Did they take Charlie in right away?" I asked.

"No," Pat said. "They gave him the chance to surrender himself at a future date at a specified time. He and Judy will have a chance to say goodbye."

"I don't know how you all have the strength to protest and go to jail and not be bitter or frightened most of your lives. You seem so calm," I said.

Pat said he planned to stop taking part in protests that could land him in prison. "My health may not permit it. I am writing about my life. I'm going to Holy Trinity to spend a few days on retreat and recollect my years as a student there."

At one point, Pat, too, had been a Trinitarian seminarian, but he left to study to become a Trappist monk in Conyers, Georgia. He was asked to leave the monastery because he was caught playing one too many tricks on the monks.

The monks would wake about 3 a.m. to sing Matins and Lauds, the Morning Prayer of the Church. Then they would have a bit of personal time. In the restrooms, there was a row of stalls, and you could tell if one was occupied if a robe dropped to the floor. Pat placed a pair of boots and robe in each stall. Any monk who tried to go to the toilet would notice they were all occupied. After a while, some of the monks got impatient and began to investigate. When they discovered the joke played on them, it was the last straw.

Pat left the seminary, studied philosophy and taught high school. He ended up joining the Army, but became a conscientious objector before his stint was over.

Pat married in California and had two children. Later, he acknowledged that he was gay and got divorced. He became a member of the Board of Supervisors in Santa Cruz County, and began protesting injustices against migrant workers. One of the supermarkets he protested against had a contest to win $1,000 a month for life. Pat, unbelievably, won.

I was happy that he would be writing about his life. I told him I was doing the same. "Richard," he said, "the hardest part of my life was the seminary at Holy Trinity and the years with the Trinitarians. That's why I am going over to Holy Trinity."

"Pat, that is exactly how I feel. I would just as soon just skip over it in my writings. One of the most difficult things for me is that I didn't agree with or like some of the men that others considered to be such good priests."

We continued to talk for a while and finally said goodbye.

Years later, in 2008, Pat suffered a stroke. The next month, he died. In an online memorial, someone described him as "the best joke teller ever." Another person said he "lit a light in Santa Cruz and woke us all up." If not for him, the person said, "the environmental movement may have remained in the dark."

Pat's life story is summed up beautifully on the site. He spent "many years seeking. Seeking truth. Seeking Peace. We who loved him all truly hope he has found that."

I miss Pat. But I occasionally talk to Charlie. He's living in California. While his days of civil disobedience have come to an end, I'm sure he's still fighting the good fight in any way he can.

CHAPTER 36

MY MOTHER AND FATHER WERE very devoted to each other. During World War II, when he left home to work in another state for three years, they wrote letters weekly. They were very kind to each other, never sarcastic or gruff. Their marriage was loving and strong. Even today, when I think of them, I think of them together.

Growing up, I never imagined myself married with children. My dreams of the future usually centered on adventures and careers. But, after I left the priesthood, I knew I wanted to marry, if I could find the right woman. I also knew I needed to wait a year before becoming involved in a romantic relationship.

From my counseling perch, I could see that many marriages failed because people lacked the skills to deal with anger or feelings of inferiority. I was filled with all kinds of emotions when I left Savannah, and I wanted a clear head before dating anyone. So I waited, and worked my issues, until the time was right.

A mutual friend thought Sandra and I would get along well. We decided to meet at a Shoney's close to my office. I arrived a little early and sat on the bench near the cash register.

A couple of times before, I had met women for coffee, but each time decided against pursuing anything other than friendship.

As I waited for Sandra to arrive, I felt nervous and cautious. I did not want to throw myself into a relationship merely as a way to heal the wounds I was still nursing.

Sandra walked in, and I introduced myself. She was blond, beautiful and smiling. One cup of coffee became several cups as we talked about our previous jobs and our upbringings. I felt comfortable with her and knew instantly that she was a special person. She was accomplished and intelligent. Before becoming an attorney, she had been a high school English teacher for many years, then decided to attend law school. For a short time, also, she had served as director of education at the local Museum of Arts and Sciences.

Our conversation turned to the Tubman Museum. I asked her if she wanted to see it, and she enthusiastically agreed. I had the keys with me, so we drove to the museum and strolled through the galleries. She was an attentive listener as I talked about the museum and how it had come to be.

It was obvious that there was a spark between us, and I knew I wanted to see her again.

I invited her to a performance by the Atlanta Symphony Orchestra, and she accepted. On that date, too, I felt at ease. It soon became clear we shared many interests, including a deep love of classical music and the arts in general.

I gave Sandra an emerald engagement ring at Christmas 1990, and we married in March at a lovely restored Victorian home. It was a very small wedding. Our honeymoon was a trip to Asheville, North Carolina.

Our lives seemed to mesh easily. Sandra embraced my old friends, like Willie Thomas, the elderly St. Peter Claver parishioner I had come to adore. Occasionally we would take Willie's large plastic bottles to Indian Springs State Park just north of Macon and fill them with water. Willie loved this spring water and deeply believed in its medicinal value.

Sometimes, Willie would come with us. In her 90s, and crippled with arthritis, she would will herself to walk from the parking lot and down at least a dozen steps to the springs.

Afterward, the three of us sometimes shared a picnic lunch at the park. Willie loved these outings, and Sandra and I loved bringing her, talking to her and learning from her.

Sandra and I recently celebrated our twenty-fifth wedding anniversary. We have prayed, laughed, cried and enjoyed countless days with her three grandchildren, whom I love as I would my own. We never tire of one another, yet give each other private time. I read somewhere that marriage is the last chance for maturity. I'm not saying this applies to everyone, but it did to me.

I know now that my sermons as a priest would have been richer and more thoughtful had I experienced married life. I have learned so much about love and acceptance from Sandra.

I've been blessed with a challenging and rewarding life. God's grace led me down a path that I'm happy I took and grateful I veered from. I have learned a lot, and I need to learn more.

My married life has been deeply rewarding. I am keenly aware that I easily could have married the wrong person. Sandra was definitely the right person. We love one another more now than when we were first married. My stepchildren, along with their spouses and children, are treasures.

I am happy for the lessons I've learned from the people I've come across in life, happy God put them in my path. I've made many mistakes, but I do not count joining the priesthood among them. I would never trade my time as a priest. And I wouldn't trade my time with Sandra. All and all, it's been a rich and fulfilling life.

Afterword

Love endures long and is slow to lose patience.
Love is kind.
Love does not envy and is not jealous.
Love does not boast and is not anxious to impress.
Love is not proud or arrogant.
Love has good manners and is not rude.
Love does not gratify self nor insist on its own way.
Love is not touchy or easily angered.
Love keeps no record of wrongs.
Love never delights in evil.
Love rejoices with the truth.
Love has no limit to its endurance.
Love always trust and is ready to believe the best.
Love never loses hope.
Love always perseveres and can outlast anything.
Love never fails nor comes to an end.

1 Corinthians 13:4-7

In the early 1960s, I was first introduced to this kind of love by someone outside of my birth family. It happened when a young white priest noticed an insecure 6-year-old girl in school at St. Peter Claver in Holy Trinity, Alabama and spoke words of love that would change her life forever. The words were so impactful that they caused this little girl to believe that there was greatness within her. That priest was Father Richard Keil and the first-grader was me, Theresa Ford.

The exact words of affirmation have escaped me over the 50-plus years that I have known Richard, but I do remember that they were words that instilled a confidence in me like never before. They caused me to believe that I didn't have to be a product of my low-income, dysfunctional upbringing. They were empowering words that gave me a hope and a future. They were words that were saturated with the love of God. I felt a father's love and approval that I had not experienced before.

In the eyes of a young girl dressed in her school-issued, faded green uniform in rural Alabama, I was amazed that a man of such stature would kneel down to speak to a scrawny, shy and frightened "colored" girl such as myself. I saw Father Keil as a powerful, white Catholic priest who was the boss of our elementary and middle schools, which were attended predominantly by poor black students. In that life-changing moment, he demonstrated what the humble, gentle, kind and reassuring love of God looks like. This love looked past what I saw in myself and chose to see the potential in me.

That was typical of Father Keil. I watched him closely over the years and saw that he was that way with everyone he encountered. He took a personal interest in the lives of most people he met. It didn't matter your background, race, creed, or color. He was the same non-threatening, loving way toward all people. It always amazed me that he took an interest in people that were outside of his own race.

He was often an advocate for those less fortunate in the world. In my young world, it was plain to see that he was a staunch supporter of civil rights and took a special interest in the well-being of African Americans. Richard taught me that love is not only colorblind, but transcends religious denominations, given that I attended Catholic schools but was raised Methodist. None of these societal barriers seemed to keep Richard from treating me, along with others, with love and respect.

Father Keil showed us that love must be courageous. It does not sit idly by and tolerate evil. In the '60s and '70s, racial inequalities abound in the south. His commitment to minorities and the attainment of their civil rights caused him to stand up against segregation and many evil forces that tried to harm and hold back the people he loved. I respect Richard today for his courage during this volatile time.

I recall him taking the teenagers from our school all the way to Panama City beach on our school bus. He exposed many of these underprivileged teens to their first encounter with a beach.

Father Keil was typically not one to be easily angered, but there was a righteous indignation in him that surfaced when others were being unfairly treated. Antithetical to his meek and non-threatening personality, he was bold and courageous, and even confrontational when necessary.

Love sees potential and believes the best in others. Father Keil knew that education was the great equalizer. This is probably why he took a personal interest in students getting a quality education not only at St. Peter Claver, but in high school and college. He opened the door and provided financial assistance for many minorities like myself to attend Pacelli High School, a Catholic school in neighboring Columbus, Georgia. Father Keil took a personal interest in our matriculation beyond high school. His fatherly love was quite evident in my life when I told him that I was going to postpone college for a year until I worked to make some money to attend later.

This did not sit well with Richard because he feared that the potential that he saw in me would wane if I didn't remain in school. He approached me after the deadlines for college applications had long passed and colleges were about to start fall classes. He firmly but lovingly told me that I had been accepted into Xavier University in Louisiana and would be attending that college in the fall. He made sure that all of the details regarding my admission were addressed.

Moreover, it didn't matter that there were no dormitory rooms available. He had already arranged for me to stay with a family for a semester until a dorm room opened up. It was not awkward for me that this family happened to be white because Richard had already taught me how to love and accept people, no matter what color. Then, and even now, he is so well-respected by many throughout the country that he is able to use these relationships for worthy causes.

Even though we lost contact for a while after I completed college, the empowerment and love for all people that Richard lived out was an integral part of me. I was able to be effective in the corporate world and eventually attended law school at the University of Georgia and worked as a successful attorney for more than 30 years in the Atlanta area. I have had great success in life because of a man who has the ability to see diamonds in the rough and has the heart to fully invest in someone's life in order to develop their potential.

Because of the sacrificial, gracious love that I have received from this meek yet powerful man over the past 50 years, my husband Walter and I have raised two confident children, Justin and Janna, who are successful in their own endeavors and are loving bridge-builders, with friends of all races, creeds and colors. This First Corinthians 13:4-7 love burns in Richard and has impacted untold lives, especially mine.

Theresa Ford Gilstrap